▼▼▼▼

The Great
CHILE
BOOK

▲▲▲▲

MARK MILLER
author of Coyote Cafe

with John Harrisson

Photography by
Lois Ellen Frank

▼▼▼▼

Ten Speed Press

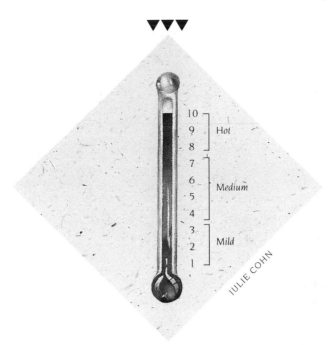

TEMPERATURE SCALE: All chiles are numbered according to this subjective heat reference, 10 being hottest and 1 being mildest.

For Elizabeth Berry, who grows wonderful chiles.

Copyright © 1991 by Mark Miller.

Special edition

Ten Speed Press
P.O. Box 7123
Berkeley, California 94707
www.tenspeed.com

Cover and text design by Fifth Street Design, Berkeley, California
Illustrations by Ellen Sasaki
Photographs by Lois Ellen Frank and Mark Miller

ISBN 1-58008-512-1

Printed in China

CONTENTS
▼▼▼

The Quest for the Enchanting Fire / 1

Chiles: A Brief Survey / 5

FRESH CHILES
(*Chiles Frescos*)

Ají 20

Ají Dulce 20

Amatista 20

Anaheim (*green*) 22

Anaheim (*red*) 24

Bell Pepper (*green*) . . . 26

Bell Pepper (*blond*) . . . 26

Bell Pepper (*orange*) . . 28

Bell Pepper (*red*) 28

Bell Pepper (*violet*) . . . 30

Bell Pepper (*yellow*) . . . 30

Brazilian Malagueta . . . 32

Chawa 32

Chilaca 34

De Agua 36

Dutch (*red*) 36

Fiesta/Fips 38

Fresno (*red*) 40

Güero 40

Habanero 42

Huachinango 44

Hungarian Cherry
  Pepper 44

Hungarian Sweet Chile . 46

Jalapeño (*green*) 48

Jalapeño (*red*) 48

Jamaican Hot 50

Korean 50

Macho (*green*) 52

Macho (*red*) 52

Manzana 52

New Mexico (*green*) . . . 54

New Mexico (*red*) 56

Peruvian 58

Peter Pepper 58

Pimento 60

Poblano (*green*) 62

Poblano (*red*) 64

Rocotillo 66

Santa Fe Grande . . . 66

Scotch Bonnet 68

Serrano 68

Sweet Purple Pepper . . 70

Tabasco 72

Tepín 72

Thai 72

DRIED CHILES
(*Chiles Secos*)

Ají Amarillo 80

Ají Mirasol 80

Ají Panca 80

Ancho 82

Cascabel 84

Catarina 84

Cayenne 86

Chilhuacle Amarillo . . . 86

Chilhuacle Negro 88

Chilhuacle Rojo 88

Chilcostle 90

Chiltepe 90

Chipotle 92

Costeño 92

Costeño Amarillo 94

De Árbol 94

Guajillo 96

Habanero 98

Hungarian Cherry
  Pepper 98

Mora 100

Morita 100

Mulato 102

New Mexico (green) . . 104

New Mexico (red) 106

New Mexico
  (NuMex Eclipse) 108

New Mexico
  (NuMex Sunrise) 110

New Mexico
  (NuMex Sunset) 112

New Mexico Miniatures 114

Onza 116

Pasado 116

Pasilla 118

Pasilla de Oaxaca . . . 120

Pátzcuaro 122

Pepperoncini 122

Pequín 124

Pico de Pajaro 124

Pulla 126

Serrano Seco 126

Serrano Seco
  de Yucatán 128

Tepín 128

Tuxtla 128

RECIPES

Chipotles In Adobo
  Sauce 135

Caribe Salsa 136

Roasted Corn Salsa . . 137

Green Chile Chutney . 138

Guajillo Salsa 139

Mark's Red Chile Sauce 140

Jalapeño Ketchup . . . 141

Green Chile Sauce . . 142

Mango-habanero Sauce 143

Smoked Chile Barbecue
  Sauce 144

Tamarind Chipotle
  Sauce 145

Pipián Rojo 146

Pipián Verde 147

Mole Rojo 148

Mole Amarillo 150

Tarascan Bean Soup . . 151

Spicy Grilled Shrimp
  and Melon Salad . . 152

Shrimp Rellenos 153

Pork Loin with Cascabel
  and Grapefruit Sauce 154

SOURCES

Fresh and Dried Chiles 155

Seeds 156

▼▼▼

THE QUEST FOR THE ENCHANTING FIRE

Chiles were not a part of my French-Canadian daily fare as I was growing up — my childhood culinary world was confined to hearty but simple foods that were prepared with a minimum of fuss. But one day, when I was about eight or nine, I ate a curry dish at the home of a family friend, and it was as though my traditional food universe was suddenly expanded and transformed. Until then, food, to me, had been one-dimensional, but the curry awakened my senses. My tongue smoked and my mouth tingled, and I discovered, through this new sensation of spiciness, that food could be colorful and exciting, alive with taste, and *fun*.

I became quite adventurous in trying different foods, and gradually came to realize there was a connection between certain foods like curries, and spicy chorizo sausages, or Szechuan Beef. Still, I didn't know what magic ingredient was responsible for these marvelous taste sensations, nor was I to learn much about it for many years. In the quasi-Puritan culture in which I grew up, it was considered impolite to discuss food: if I asked what made these dishes so interesting and different, the answers were too general. And even if I'd known what to look for, I'm sure our local grocery store wouldn't have stocked the foreign ingredients so common to the supermarkets of today.

▼▼

It wasn't until I moved to Berkeley, where I was attending the University of California, that I began to close in on my quarry. For the first time in my life, I had to prepare my own food, and in doing so, I opened myself to a whole new world. I began to experiment with various cuisines, taking advantage of all the readily available authentic ethnic ingredients. I haunted the many ethnic food neighborhoods of San Francisco, such as Chinatown, the Italian section of North Beach, and Japantown, as well as the great produce markets in that city. In doing so, I was exposed to all kinds of cuisines and experienced endless varieties of flavors, textures, preparations, and ways of eating. Across this landscape of exotic ingredients I reencountered and recognized an old friend that had awakened my senses so long ago.

My chosen field of study — anthropology — led me to travel, and it dovetailed perfectly with my culinary interest. I could learn about the fascinating foods of different cultures and then taste them in their original settings. As I visited countries such as Mexico, Guatemala, Trinidad, Thailand, Morocco, and Hungary, I was particularly excited and captivated by the sights and smells of the markets, and by the tastes and aromas of the expressive foods. Upon returning from these journeys, I would attempt to duplicate the dishes I had most recently experienced and try them on willing friends who shared my excitement for new taste sensations.

Of course I had long since identified the ingredient that had so enchanted and mystified me as a child. In fact, it had become my closest ally and friend. My efforts to understand this ingredient's many qualities have provided me with a constant source of inspiration and expression. It brings life to the food I enjoy. It is part of the foundation for my culinary creativity.

I decided to move closer to the home of this magical ingredient, so I settled in New Mexico, where its spirit hangs in the air and pervades the shadows. And now, reflecting on the 30 years in which I have searched for the identity of that fiery, tingling sensation I experienced as a youngster, I have found more answers than I could ever have imagined. The lifetime friend whose company I enjoy so much is the enchanting spirit with innumerable faces that is known to us as the chile.

This book is written to commemorate my lifelong friendship with chiles. It is my sincere hope that this book will help others to unravel the mystery that I have spent so many years trying to fully comprehend and that it will help others appreciate the many facets of this unique ingredient that can be playful or serious, young or old, subtle or obvious, complex and sensuous.

More Chiles!

Mark Miller

CHILES:
A BRIEF SURVEY

The world of chiles is as bewildering as it is fascinating. There are as many as 150 to 200 different varieties of chiles that have been positively identified. In addition, there are undoubtedly some rare varieties growing in remote regions of Mexico or South America that have yet to be discovered, and new ones that are being developed by plant geneticists even now. Add to this the fact that chiles are widely spread and they cross-breed freely and you can appreciate the impossibility of coming up with a definitive listing of chiles.

That was never my plan, anyway: this book was not intended to be an exhaustive field guide. Instead I wanted to share what I've learned about chiles from a culinary standpoint. I wanted to create a book that would help the amateur chef come to terms with genus *Capsicum* by providing full-scale photographs, detailed descriptions of appearance and taste, and advice on how to use it in cooking. The book identifies those chiles most commonly available in the United States, Mexico, and Europe, as well as most of the South American chiles and a number of rare exotics. The chiles that have not been included are not commonly available and, in any event, have similar flavors and characteristics as others listed here. It would be possible to make any recipe in the world that includes chiles and find in this book either the variety called for or an appropriate substitute.

This book also aims to clarify some of the confusion that surrounds chiles. Much of this confusion stems from the fact that many chiles are known by different names in different localities. For example, the *poblano* chile is referred to as the *pasilla* in California and parts of the Southwest, whereas the pasilla is, in fact, the dried form of a completely different chile, the *chilaca*. Sometimes different chiles go by the same name because they are similar in appearance. For example, red Fresno chiles are sometimes mistakenly labeled as red jalapeños because they are similar in shape, size, and color. However, the red Fresno is a distinct variety with a more pronounced heat. Fresh Anaheim chiles and New Mexico green chiles are also frequently confused. They look very much alike, but were bred for different flavor characteristics — the Anaheim generally being much milder, the New Mexico being hotter and more refined. Dried *ancho* and *mulato* chiles are often mislabeled in stores, too. (Mislabeling is a common problem, by the way, so don't always rely on what's written on packages or bins!)

Even the spelling of the word *chile* gets confusing, as it variously appears as *chili* and as *chilli*. These alternate spellings depend on how the word is used, on which part of the country you're in, and even on personal whim! The general convention for proper usage is that *chile* refers to the plant or pod, while *chili* refers to the traditional dish containing meat and chiles (and sometimes beans), and *chilli* is the commercial spice powder that contains ground chiles along with a number of other seasonings. But don't count on it! (The Nahuatl Indians who inhabited southern Mexico and Central America around the 15th century called the plant *chilli*, and that is the true origin of the word, no matter how you spell it.)

Another confusion dates back to that same period, when Columbus discovered the capsicum and thought he'd found the plant that produces black pepper (actually, true pepper is genus *piper nigrum*, and bears no relationship to chiles). Nevertheless, he christened it "pepper," and that misnomer has persisted ever since, particularly in Europe.

The first chiles were tiny wild berries that grew on vines beneath the forest canopy of the Amazon jungle in South America thousands of years ago. The plants proliferated and gradually spread northwards from central South America through Central America, the Caribbean, and into southwestern North America. This continued migration was the result both of birds spreading the seeds and of cultural exchanges and trade between the peoples of South America and Mesoamerica.

Chiles were one of the earliest plants to be cultivated and domesticated in the New World (other early crops were beans, corn, and squash). Archaeological evidence suggests that chiles were used as a food ingredient at least 8,000 years ago — around 6200 B.C. Traces of chiles dating from this time have been found in burial sites in Peru: they were obviously seen as important enough to be carried into the hereafter!

Chiles were used in the pre-Columbian New World to impart flavor and spiciness to food. They were common to the diets of the civilizations of the Incas, Olmecs, Toltecs, Mayans, and Aztecs, among others. The Mayans cultivated many types of chile (at least 30 varieties have been identified) and recent evidence shows that the Aztecs used them in almost every dish. The sophisticated cuisine of the Aztecs, which included mole and pipián

▼▼

sauces and tamales, and which, in turn, was derived from other pre-Columbian civilizations, laid the foundations for modern Mexican food.

It is also virtually certain that chiles were grown and used in what is now the United States by the ancestors of today's Southwestern Pueblo Indians some 1,000 years ago. It is known that wild chiles similar to the *chiltepín* grew in the Sonoran desert and were gathered by those tribes. In addition, inter-tribal trade brought other type of chiles to them from regions to the south.

The Spanish colonization of the Southwest and the foundation of the Mission system, which fostered the development of agriculture, were important factors in the rapid spread of chiles throughout that region. In the 16th century, for instance, the Spanish explorer Captain General Juan de Oñate introduced the formal cultivation of certain varieties from Mexico.

At the time of Columbus's "discovery" of "pepper," black pepper was a highly prized commodity, as valuable as silver in the European marketplace. Columbus's mistake was a happy one though, for he and other explorers brought chile seeds back to their homelands, and the fruit from the plants of these seeds received a rousing reception. Chiles were found to be a good substitute for black pepper; they added a welcome piquancy and flavor to the existing cuisines. They were also easy to grow whereas true pepper is not.

The Spanish and Portuguese explorers took chiles with them on their travels, and the plant rapidly established itself along the new maritime trade routes to North Africa, the West African coast, Madagascar, and India. The native populations there incorporated chiles into their diets, and chiles soon became a part of the cuisines of those regions. By 1550, chiles had reached western China, Southeast Asia, and the East Indies. Within 100 years, then, chiles had spread from the Americas right around the world. They had even reached such far-flung, landlocked countries as Hungary (brought there by the Ottoman Turks), and Tibet.

Today, chiles are grown throughout the world, but the major portion of the world's crop is grown (and eaten) in Mexico. They are also widely grown in New Mexico (the largest producer of chiles in the United States), California, Texas, and Arizona. Louisiana is also a major producer, probably because chiles are an integral part of the Creole and Cajun cuisines, not to mention the fact that Louisiana is the home of several well-known hot chile sauces. Chiles are being grown increasingly in other parts of the United States as interest in ethnic foods and spicier dishes has grown.

Often, particular varieties of chiles are grown only in particular regions or localities. Usually this is a matter of suitable growing conditions (soil make-up and quality, climate, etc.) — *habanero* chiles will not grow in the mountains of northern New Mexico, yet they prosper 250 miles away at a lower altitude in a longer growing season. Sometimes it has more to do with cultural or historical factors; these apply particularly to a number of chiles grown in the Yucatán and Oaxaca regions of Mexico.

In general, though, chiles are easy to grow. They require only a small area for cultivation and minimal care. They can be grown almost anywhere in the United States, although they do best in warm, humid climates with a long growing season (in tropical regions, they are treated as perennials). The foliage is lush and the plant fruit is attractive enough in some

▼▼

cases to be grown for ornamental purposes. Many varieties make excellent container plants and thrive indoors as houseplants.

Chile plants are prolific, so five or six plants will probably do for one family, in which case you would buy seedlings at the nursery in the spring. To start them from seed you would want to get an 8- to 10-week head start and set the plants out when all danger of frost is past. Seed sources are listed on page 156.

Chiles cross-pollinate freely so that different types should be grown separately to reduce the possibility of producing hybrids. This could result in hotter chiles increasing the potency of adjacent milder chiles, or vice versa. Incidentally, the chile pods on any one plant can vary in hotness.

I've been asked whether it is feasible to dry your own chiles. I usually advise against this because, unless you live in an area with very low humidity, you will need a commercial dryer or else the chiles will rot. However, if you have a bumper crop and want to try, consult Sunset Magazine or a similar reference for information on the proper techniques.

Chiles are available commercially in a number of forms: fresh, dried, frozen, canned, and powdered. At Coyote Cafe we use some 20 different types of fresh chiles, including Anaheims, Fresnos, New Mexico greens and reds, *poblanos*, *serranos*, jalapeños, *habaneros*, Thais, Hungarian cherry peppers, and sweet peppers. We use about the same number of dried chiles, mainly in sauces. The varieties we use most frequently are *anchos*, *chipotles*, *cascabels*, *de árbols*, *mulatos*, *guajillos*, *pequíns*, and New Mexico reds.

When a recipe calls for fresh chiles and none are available, commercially frozen chiles are the next best thing. My preference is for the more flavorful New Mexican green chiles. These are generally available only in the Southwest, however, or through mail order sources.

Except for chipotle chiles in adobo sauce or pickled chiles (*chiles en escabeche*), you should avoid canned chiles as their flavor tends to be tinny and the consistency mushy. They are too flimsy for stuffing as rellenos although they can be sliced and used as a topping for burgers or diced and used in salsas or stuffings. Canned chiles are best rinsed before use.

Pure chile powder, made exclusively from one type of chile, is traditionally used in making chile sauces and as a seasoning for everything from tamales to pasta and breads. You will most likely find the freshest (and cheapest) chile powders in Latin American markets. A good quality chile powder should have a deep rich color and should not be too powdery or dry. A slightly lumpy consistency indicates that the natural oils have not evaporated and are still fresh. These oils contain the essential flavors and should leave a stain when a little chile powder is rubbed between the fingers. The aroma should be strong, intense, and earthy. Avoid buying commercial chile powder mixes that contain black pepper, salt, sugar, cumin, garlic powder, and paprika, but very little real chile powder, which is the essential ingredient.

The characteristic for which chiles are best known is their heat. This fiery sensation is caused by capsaicin, a potent chemical that survives both cooking and freezing processes. The amount of capsaicin present in a chile determines its fieriness. In addition to causing a burning sensation, this substance triggers the brain to produce endorphins, natural painkillers that promote a sense of well-being and stimulation.

▼▼

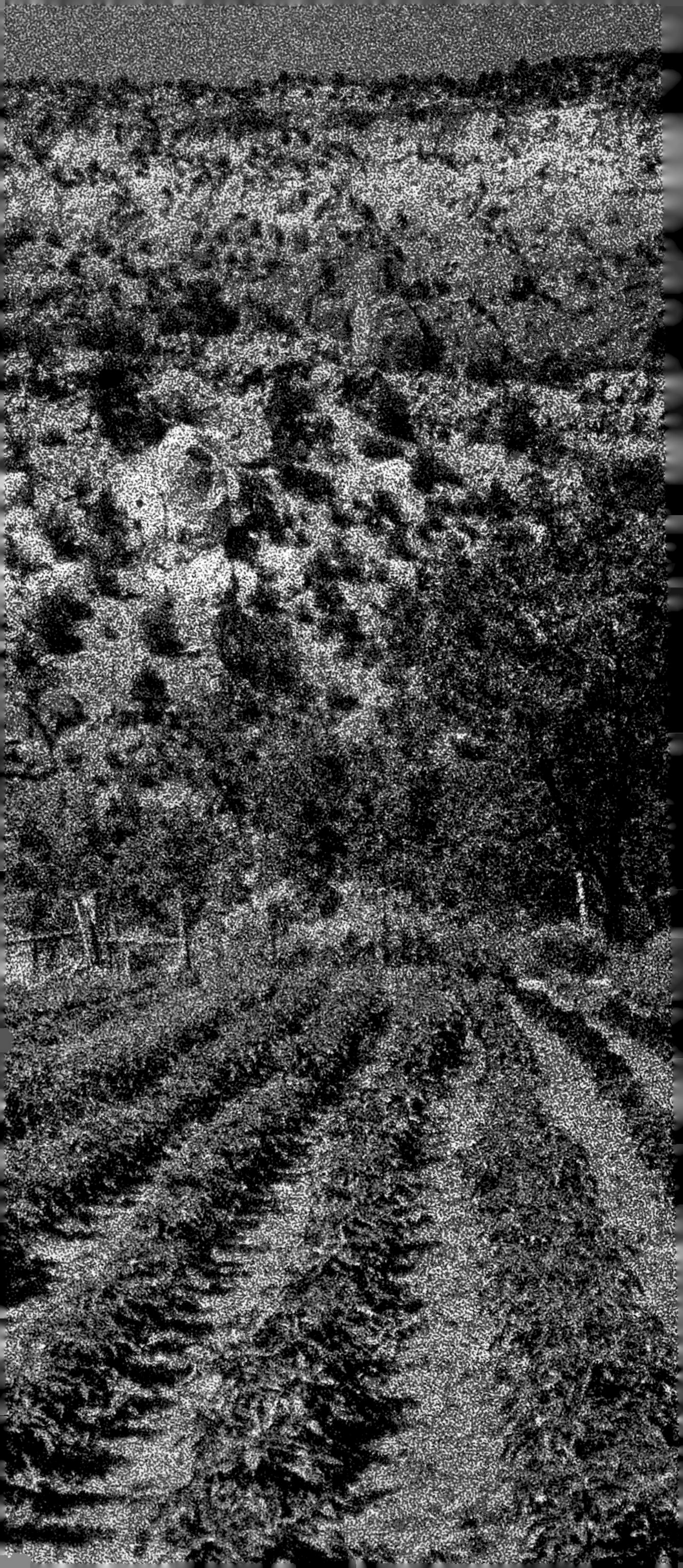

FRESH
Fresco

FRESH CHILES
(*Chiles Frescos*)

Most chiles are green in color while they are growing and still in their unripened state. When they ripen and reach their full maturity, almost all of them turn to shades of red, orange, yellow, or brown. Many chiles are used both green and fully ripened, as you will see. In those cases a color may be tacked onto the name just for purposes of description and not to denote a different species — the New Mexico green and New Mexico red, for instance, are the same chile in different stages of ripeness. (To avoid confusion, try to learn the Spanish words for the most common chile colors: *rojo* means red; *verde* means green; *negro* means black, and *amarillo* means yellow. *Colorado* also denotes a reddish hue.) In general, the redder the chile (and therefore, the riper), the sweeter and fruitier it is, and the broader the shoulders, the milder it is.

When buying fresh chiles, select those that are mature, dry, firm, and heavy for their size. The skin should be shiny, smooth, and unblemished, and the chile should have a fresh, clean smell. Wash the chiles to remove dirt or other residue, dry them, wrap them in paper towels, and store them in the crisper section of your refrigerator, where they should keep for up to two or three weeks. Do not store them in plastic bags as moisture will accumulate and hasten the spoiling process, and don't leave them out in the open as they will shrivel and rapidly lose flavor and texture.

If you are at all sensitive to capsaicin, it is best to wear rubber gloves when preparing chiles, especially the hotter varieties (those over 6 on our heat scale). If you handle (and eat) chiles over a long period of time, your fingers (and taste buds) will get increasingly used to the capsaicin contained in chiles. Still, you should exercise caution: be particularly careful not to touch your face or eyes when working with chiles and wash your hands thoroughly when you are done.

It is common in many cuisines, including Southwestern and Mexican cooking, to roast or grill fresh chiles and peel them before further use. The skin, if left on, can give off a bitter flavor. Roasting makes it easier to remove the skin, and also seems to bring out a fuller chile flavor, transforming the green, vegetable tones of the "raw" chile and giving it a distinctive earthy, smoky flavor. I find that following such traditional cooking techniques brings an added dimension to the cooking and dining experience.

Fresh chiles should be roasted quickly and evenly on a rack over an open gas flame, under a broiler, or on a grill. You want to blister and blacken the skin all over without burning through the flesh. One of the best ways I've found to do this is to use an inexpensive hand-held butane torch, available from good hardware stores. Roast the chiles quickly or the flesh may fall apart and lose shape. Don't even try to roast chiles unless they are firm and fresh. (An alternative to roasting is to dip fresh chiles in hot oil for about a minute to blister the skins. This method is preferable if you are using the chiles in dishes with delicate flavors — seafood salads, for example — where the smoky roasted flavor could prove overpowering.)

After roasting, the chiles should then be placed in a bowl, covered with a clean kitchen towel or plastic wrap, and allowed to "sweat" and cool. The skin can then be easily pulled off with your fingers or the edge of a knife. Do not wash roasted chiles under running water as you will dilute the natural oils and hence the delicious, smoky flavor. Split the chiles open and scoop out the seeds and pith with the tip of a knife, and remove the stem (unless you're preparing a chile relleno). Chiles can be roasted ahead of time and kept in the refrigerator for one or two days.

One of my favorite chile flavors is that of the roasted poblano, peeled and cut into thin strips or *rajas*. Rajas can be added to salads, soups, or tacos. I also like the flavor of smoked fresh chiles and use them to enhance everything from sauces to soups and salads. It gives them that special taste of the outdoors. If you have a smoker, you can smoke chiles at home. Use a sweet fruit wood, such as apple, and smoke the chiles for about 40 minutes.

In cooking, I use fresh chiles primarily for flavor accents. At the same time, I take into consideration their heat, texture, and color. Fresh chiles vary widely in heat, acidity, and citrus quality, and should be used accordingly. For example, the habanero with its lively taste reminiscent of mango or papaya and its hot, clear qualities is probably my most favorite chile of all. It, and its close relative, the Scotch bonnet, will pick up the flavors of a tropical salsa by reinforcing the fruity tropical tones. Serranos, with their sharper green accents, go particularly well with tomatoes and cilantro and would be my choice for a dish that contains those ingredients. If you are using roasted chiles to make a sauce, try using a blend of two or three compatible types instead of a single variety. For example, poblanos, jalapeños, and serranos complement each other well, and combining them adds a pleasing complexity to a sauce. This is something you can experiment with as you become more comfortable cooking with chiles.

▼▼

AJÍ

Although it is usually seen in its yellow dried form (see *ají mirasol* in the dried chile section), the *ají* can also be found in its green or red state. It tapers to a point, and measures about 3 to 5 inches long and ¾ inch in diameter. Thin fleshed; has a tropical fruit flavor and a searing, clear heat. Used in ceviches, salsas, and sauces, and pickled (en escabeche).

AJÍ DULCE

Related to the habanero and Scotch bonnet. Bright green to yellow, orange, and red. Shaped like a miniature elongated bell pepper. Measures about 2 to 3 inches long and 1½ to 2 inches in diameter. Thin fleshed; very fruity in flavor and hot. This is not, as the name suggests, a sweet or mild chile. Used in tropical salsas and fish stews.

AMATISTA

An ornamental. Bright purple, with wide shoulders tapering to a rounded end, measuring about ½ to 1½ inches long and ½ inch in diameter. Thick fleshed; has earthy, deep, sweet (but not fruity) tones. Commonly pickled (en escabeche), and used decoratively in salads.

AJÍ
Source: South America, especially Peru. Heat: 7-8

AJÍ DULCE
Source: Venezuela and northeastern South America. Heat: 7-8.5

AMATISTA
Source: South America. Heat: 7

ANAHEIM
(*green*)

Also known as the California or long green chile, and closely related to the New Mexico chile. Pale to medium bright green, tapered, and measuring about 6 inches long and 2 to 2½ inches in diameter. Medium to thick fleshed; has a green vegetable flavor that is improved by roasting. Originally grown around Anaheim in Southern California at the turn of the twentieth century. Now available year-round in California and the Southwest, and in Latin markets elsewhere. Excellent stuffed (rellenos). Also used in stews and sauces, and as rajas.

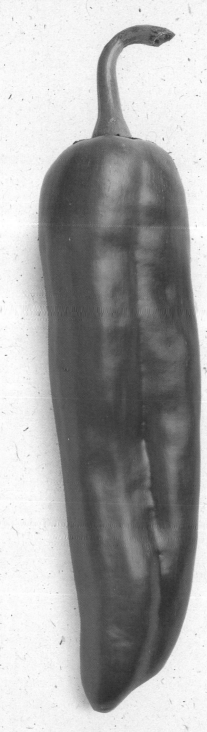

ANAHEIM (*green*)

Source: California and the Southwest. Heat: 2-3

ANAHEIM
(*red*)

Ripe form of the green Anaheim. Also known as the *chile colorado* or long red chile. The red Anaheim has a more developed sweetness than the green Anaheim and is a very versatile chile. Excellent in sauces, as rajas, and stuffed (rellenos). Also good pickled (en escabeche) and grilled. Used as a decorative element in soups and stews. Dried red Anaheims are commonly used to make ristras. The powdered form is also sold as *chile colorado*.

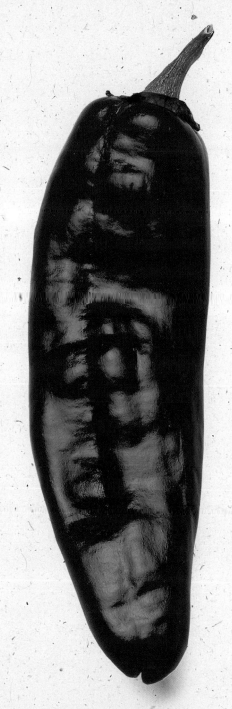

ANAHEIM (*red*)
Source: California and the Southwest. Heat: 2-3

BELL PEPPER
(*green*)

Bright medium green, shaped like a
cube but rounded at the edges,
sometimes tapering slightly from
broad shoulders. Measures about 4
to 5 inches long and about 3 to 4
inches in diameter. Thick fleshed;
has a sweet, mild, green vegetable
flavor. Never substitute bell peppers
for chiles such as Anaheims or New
Mexico greens or reds in Southwestern or Latin American dishes, as
the flavors are not complementary
to the spices used. Bell peppers also
occur in a variety of other colors.
Used in salads, casseroles, and in
vegetable dishes. Can be stuffed,
roasted, or grilled.

BELL PEPPER
(*blond*)

White to pale yellow bell pepper,
measuring about the same as the
green bell pepper. Thick fleshed; not
as sweet as the red or yellow bell
peppers. Mainly used decoratively.

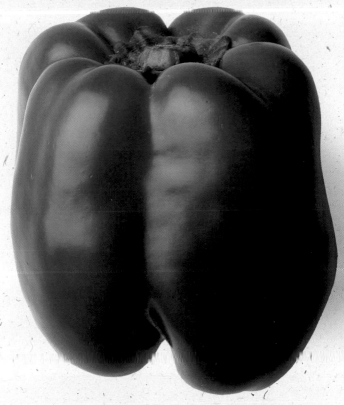

BELL PEPPER (*green*)

Primary Sources: Mediterranean Basin, Mexico, and
California. Heat: 0

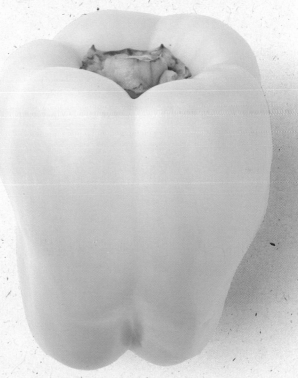

BELL PEPPER (*blond*)

Source: Holland. Heat: 0

BELL PEPPER
(*orange*)

Bright orange, slightly smaller than the green bell pepper, measuring about 3 to 4 inches long and 3 inches in diameter. Thick fleshed; very sweet, with crisp, fruity tones. Used in salads, salsas, and stews, and with pastas. Can be grilled or roasted.

BELL PEPPER
(*red*)

Also known as a sweet red pepper. Bright red, usually shaped like the green bell pepper, measuring about 4 to 5 inches long and 3 to 4 inches in diameter. Thick fleshed; very sweet, with crisp, fruity tones similar to ripened tomatoes. Used in salads and stews, and with pastas. Can be grilled or roasted.

BELL PEPPER (*orange*)
Source: Holland and California. Heat: 0

BELL PEPPER (*red*)
Source: Holland, the Mediterranean Basin, and California.
Heat: 0

BELL PEPPER
(*violet*)

Bright medium purple to violet, tapered, measuring about 5 to 6 inches long and 3 inches in diameter. Thick fleshed; very sweet, though not quite as sweet as the red, orange, or yellow bell peppers. This pepper darkens a little when cooked. Used as a decorative element in salads. Can be roasted.

BELL PEPPER
(*yellow*)

Bright yellow, similar in size and shape to the green bell pepper. Thick fleshed; very sweet, with crisp, fruity tones. Used in salads, and salsas, and with pastas. Can be grilled or roasted.

BELL PEPPER (*violet*)
Source: Holland. Heat: 0

BELL PEPPER (*yellow*)
Source: Holland, the Mediterranean Basin, and California.
Heat: 0

BRAZILIAN MALAGUETA

Light to medium green, tapered, and measuring ¾ to 1 inch long and about ¼ to ½ inch in diameter. Thin fleshed; a searing heat with a slightly green flavor. Often added to marinades and vinegars; also pickled (en escabeche).

CHAWA

Pale to medium yellow, usually curved and tapering to a point, measuring about 3 to 5 inches long and 1 to 1½ inches in diameter. Very thin fleshed; has a sweet, mild flavor. Very similar in appearance and characteristics to the banana or Hungarian wax chiles, which are marketed mostly in California in the fall. Most commonly used in salads and ceviches, or pickled (en escabeche). Can also be used for stuffing (cold rellenos).

BRAZILIAN MALAGUETA
Source: Brazil. Heat: 9

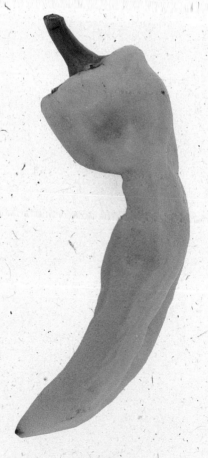

CHAWA
Source: Yucatán and the Caribbean coastal area of Mexico.
Heat: 3-4

CHILACA

Dark brown or chocolate colored, elongated, and often curving in shape. Measures about 6 to 9 inches long and 1 inch in diameter. Most often used in its dried form, when it is referred to as a *chile pasilla* or *chile negro*. Very rarely found fresh in North America. Sometimes pickled (en escabeche) or added to sauces.

CHILACA

Source: Guanajuato, Jalisco, and
Zacatecas (central Mexico).
Heat: 3-4

DE AGUA

Medium green to red when fully ripe. Tapered to a point, and measuring about 4 to 5 inches long and 1 to 1½ inches in diameter. Thin fleshed; has a green, vegetable flavor, a little sharp like a tomatillo, with little fruitiness. The red *de agua* has a more developed sweetness than the green. Excellent stuffed (rellenos), or used in soups or mole sauces.

DUTCH (*red*)

Also known as the Holland chile. Bright scarlet, slightly curved, and tapering to a point. Measures about 4 inches long and 1 to 1½ inches in diameter. Thick fleshed; has a sweet, hot, and intense flavor. This chile is a new hybrid cultivar developed for the booming Dutch export trade in specialty produce. It was probably bred from an Indonesian variety. It can be substituted for the red Thai chile or the red Fresno chile. Commonly used in salsas and as a decorative element in soups and stews. It can be roasted and blended into sauces and can also be pickled (en escabeche).

DE AGUA
Source: Oaxaca region.
Heat: 4.5

DUTCH (*red*)
Source: Holland. Heat: 6

FIESTA / FIPS

Both these ornamentals are related to the cayenne and Tabasco chiles. There are many similar ornamentals, varying in color from bright deep red or scarlet to a cream, yellow, or orange. Usually cylindrical and slightly tapered, with a rounded end. Measures about 1 to 2 inches long and ½ to ¾ inches in diameter. These chiles vary in flavor from mild to sweet and intense. They grow well indoors in small pots, and can be used as a table decoration. Although they are mainly decorative, they can be used in cooking to add a little zip to salsas, stews, and stir-fries.

FIESTA / FIPS

Source: Northern Mexico and Louisiana. Heat: 6-8

FRESNO (*red*)

Also known as a *chile caribe* or *chile cera*. Tapers to a rounded end and measures about 2 inches long and between 1 to 1¼ inches in diameter. A wax-type chile, thick fleshed, sweet, and hot. Usually only available in the fall. It is sometimes mistaken for a red jalapeño, although the two are different varieties and the Fresno is broader at the shoulders, as well as hotter. Excellent in salsas, ceviches, stuffings, breads, and pickled (en escabeche). They can also be roasted and blended into sauces.

GÜERO

Güero is a generic term for yellow chiles, the name coming from the Spanish, meaning light skinned or blond. It usually applies to pale yellow tapered chiles such as the Hungarian wax or banana chiles, or the Santa Fe grande. Size varies from about 3 to 5 inches long and 1 to 1½ inches in diameter. Medium fleshed, slightly sweet, with a sharp and intense waxy taste. Varies in strength from medium to hot. Primarily used to make yellow mole sauces. Can also be used in other sauces or in salads, or pickled (en escabeche).

FRESNO (red)
Source: Mexico, California, and the Southwest. Heat: 6.5

GÜERO
Source: Northern Mexico and the Southwest. Heat: 4.5-6.5

HABANERO

Dark green to orange, orange-red, or red when fully ripe. Lantern shaped, and measuring about 2 inches long and 1¼ to 1¾ inches in diameter. The habanero (meaning "from Havana") is used extensively in the Yucatán and is the hottest of any chile grown in Central America or the Caribbean, and indeed, the rest of the world. Users beware! It has been estimated that the habanero is 30 to 50 times hotter than the jalapeño, and it can have an irritating effect in the mouth and on the fingers. Be careful when handling. In spite of its fierce, intense heat, it has a wonderful, distinctive flavor with tropical fruit tones that mix well with food containing tropical fruits or tomatoes. The ripe habanero is a little sweeter and has a more developed fruitiness than the green habanero. Closely related to the Scotch bonnet and the Jamaican hot chiles. Mainly used in salsas, chutneys, marinades for seafood, and pickled (en escabeche). It is becoming increasingly popular in the United States as a bottled condiment sauce.

HABANERO
Source: Yucatán and the Caribbean. Heat: 10

HUACHINANGO

Region-specific name in central Mexico, Puebla, and Oaxaca for a type of large red jalapeño. Commonly found with white veins on the skin, tapers to a rounded end and measures about 4 to 5 inches long and about 1½ inches in diameter. Thick fleshed; sweet, with a medium-hot intensity. They are highly prized for their sweetness and thick flesh, and cost three to four times as much as common jalapeños. *Huachinango* chiles are smoked and dried to make *chipotle grande* chiles (see *Chipotle* in the dried chile section). Fresh huachinango chiles are commonly used in salsas, stews and sauces.

HUNGARIAN CHERRY PEPPER

Scarlet to deep red in color, almost spherical, and measuring about 1¾ inches in diameter. Fleshy, with many seeds. Has medium sweetness and is usually mild, but can range to medium in heat. Similar in shape to the hotter Creole pepper. Most commonly used in salads, and pickled (en escabeche). Sometimes dried.

HUACHINANGO

*Source: Oaxaca, Puebla, and the central valley of Mexico
(Mexico City region). Heat: 5-6*

HUNGARIAN CHERRY PEPPER

Source: Hungary, Eastern Europe, and California. Heat: 1-3

HUNGARIAN SWEET CHILE

Deep crimson, elongated, with broad shoulders and a rounded end, measuring 5 to 6 inches long and about 2 to 2½ inches in diameter at the shoulders. Thick fleshed; very sweet. Similar in flavor to the pimento. Can be roasted and stuffed or used in sauces.

HUNGARIAN SWEET CHILE

Source: Hungary, Eastern Europe, and California. Heat: 0-1

JALAPEÑO (*green*)

Named after the town of Jalapa in the Mexican state of Veracruz. Bright medium to dark green, tapering to a rounded end, and measuring about 2 to 3 inches long and 1 to 1½ inches in diameter. Thick fleshed; has a green vegetable flavor. Probably the best known and most widely eaten hot chile in the United States, and the first chile to be taken to space, in 1982. Jalapeños can be added to almost anything that you want to spice up: salsas, stews, breads, sauces, dips, etc. They can be diced up and used as a topping for snack foods. They are also good pickled (en escabeche), or roast them and stuff them with cheese, fish, or meat to be served as a cocktail snack.

JALAPEÑO (*red*)

Ripe form of the green jalapeño. The red jalapeño has a sweeter flavor than the green. Use it pickled (en escabeche) or in salsas, stews, sauces, or tamales. It can also be served as rajas, or roasted for soups. Red jalapeños are dried by smoking them, usually over mesquite wood. The dried smoked jalapeños are known as *chipotle* chiles.

JALAPEÑO (*green*)

Source: Veracruz, Oaxaca, Chihuahua, Texas, and other
parts of the Southwest. Heat: 5.5

JALAPEÑO (*red*)

Source: Veracruz, Oaxaca, Chihuahua, Texas, and other
parts of the Southwest. Heat: 5.5

JAMAICAN HOT

Related to the habanero and Scotch bonnet. Bright red, smaller than the habanero but similar in shape, about 2 inches long and 1 to 1½ inches in diameter. Very thin fleshed, with a sweet, hot flavor. The Jamaican hot is particularly suited to dishes containing tropical fruits. Commonly used in salsas, Caribbean fish stews, curries, and chutneys.

KOREAN

Related to the Thai chile. Bright green, slightly curved, and tapering to a point. Measures about 3 to 4 inches long and about ¾ inches in diameter. Very thin fleshed, with a hot green vegetable flavor. Available at Korean or Southeast Asian grocery stores. Grown in the United States for the Korean community. This is the chile that gives the heat to kim chee, the spicy Korean pickled relish. It is also used in marinades and other pickled dishes.

JAMAICAN HOT
Source: Jamaica and other Caribbean islands. Heat: 9

KOREAN
Source: Korea, Japan, and California. Heat: 6-7

MACHO (*green*)

Related to the *pequín*. Light to medium green, and measuring about ¼ inch or less. Use sparingly — this is a small but mighty chile, as you might guess by its name. It is fiery hot, with a very sharp, intense flavor, and green tones. Mainly used in salsas. Can also be used in stews: add the whole chiles and remove them before serving.

MACHO (red)

Ripe form of the green *macho*. Slightly larger, and with sweeter, riper tones. Like the green macho, it is commonly used in salsas and stews. The red macho chile is often grown as a small potted ornamental.

MANZANA

Also known as *chile rocoto*, *chile perón*, or *chile caballo*. Usually yellow-orange, and shaped very much like a bell pepper, measuring about 3 inches long and 2 to 2¼ inches in diameter. Thin fleshed; soft and meaty in texture, with fruitlike flavors. Usually medium-hot, but can be very hot. The *manzana* is unusual in that its seeds are black. Used in salsas and sauces, or stuffed (rellenos). It is also sliced into rajas and added to other dishes or served alone as a vegetable.

MACHO (*green*)

Source: Oaxaca and Yucatán regions. Heat: 9-10

MACHO (*red*)

Source: Oaxaca and Yucatán regions. Heat: 9-10

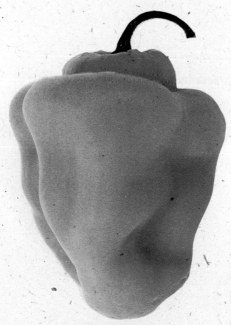

MANZANA

Source: Central America, Michoacán, and the central valley
of Mexico (Mexico City region). Heat: 6-8

▼▼▼

NEW MEXICO (*green*)

Also known as the long green chile.
Pale to medium green, tapered, and
measuring between 6 to 9 inches
long and about 1 ½ to 2 inches in
diameter. Medium fleshed; varies
considerably in strength from medium to very hot. The flavor is unlike
that of any other chile in North
America: sweet and earthy, with a
clarity that seems to reflect the skies
and landscapes of New Mexico. It is
hotter and has a clearer, more cut-
ting chile flavor than the Anaheim. It
is available fresh almost year-round,
although anyone who has been to
Santa Fe in the fall knows that these
chiles are roasted in huge quantities
at that time of year when the bulk of
the crop is in. They freeze well, and
frozen New Mexico green chiles are
better than canned. The New Mexico
green is excellent in green chile
sauces, stews, and salsas, stuffed
(rellenos), and as rajas. Try them
roasted and peeled in sandwiches.
In most cases, you can substitute a
mixture of Anaheims and roasted
jalapeños if the New Mexico greens
are unavailable.

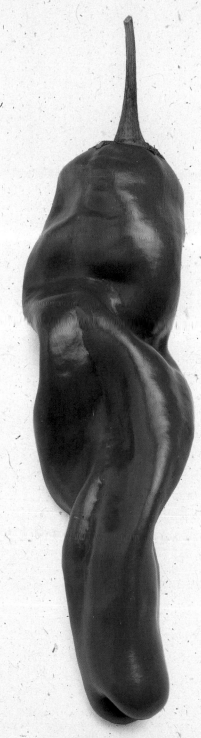

NEW MEXICO (*green*)
Source: Rio Grande Valley (New Mexico). Heat: 3-5

NEW MEXICO
(*red*)

Ripe form of the New Mexico green chile. A dark, intense red; fleshy and sweet. The New Mexico red varies from medium to medium-hot. When roasted, peeled, and dried, referred to as a *chile pasado* (rarely found in this form outside New Mexico). Commonly roasted and used in red chile sauces, barbecue sauces, pipián sauces, chutneys, salsas, rellenos, and tamales. They are also good as rajas.

NEW MEXICO (*red*)
Source: Rio Grande Valley (New Mexico). Heat: 3-4

PERUVIAN

Green, yellow, or red, rounded in shape, and measuring about 2½ inches long and about 1½ inches in diameter. Thin fleshed; has a fruity taste with tropical berry tones. Primarily used in salsas and ceviches.

PETER PEPPER

Ripe form of a rare ornamental. Bright red and crinkled, measuring about 3 to 4 inches long and about 1 inch in diameter. Medium to thick fleshed, with a sweet, hot flavor. Mainly an ornamental, but can be used in salsas.

PERUVIAN
Source: Peru, Columbia, and Venezuela.
Heat: 7-8

PETER PEPPER
Source: Louisiana and Texas. Heat: 7.5

PIMENTO

Also known as *chile pimiento, pimiento dulce*, and *pimiento morrón*. Scarlet, almost heart shaped, tapering to a point, and measuring about
4 inches long and 2½ to 3 inches in diameter. Fleshy and wonderfully sweet and aromatic, this chile is more flavorful than the red bell pepper, and varies in strength from very mild to slightly hot. It is most commonly used in its powdered form which is called paprika. The best paprika is imported from Hungary. Look for it in the gourmet section of your grocery store or in shops that specialize in imported food items. Fresh pimentos are good in salads. Canned pimentos are most often used as garnishes.

PIMENTO

*Source: California, southern United States, Hungary,
and Spain.* Heat: 1

POBLANO (*green*)

One of the most popular fresh chiles used in Mexico. Dark green, with a purple-black tinge, tapering down from the shoulders to a point. Measures about 4 to 5 inches long and 2½ to 3 inches in diameter. Thick fleshed; varies in strength between medium and hot. It is mistakenly referred to as a *pasilla* in California, even though the pasilla is a different type of chile altogether (see Pasilla in the dried chile section). The green poblano is always used cooked or roasted and never eaten raw. Roasting gives the poblano a fuller, smoky, more earthy flavor. Poblanos that are very fiery should be seeded and deveined. This chile is favored for making chiles rellenos or any other stuffed chile dish because of its size and the thickness of the flesh. Also good as rajas, or made into sauces, especially moles and pipiáns.

POBLANO (*green*)

Source: *Puebla region, central valley of Mexico (Mexico City region), and California.* Heat: 3

POBLANO
(*red*)

Ripe form of the green poblano.
Deep red-brown in color, and
sweeter than the green. In its dried
form it is known as an ancho chile or
a mulato chile. Best roasted and
used for rellenos or rajas. Also good
in soups, stews, tamales, and sauces.

POBLANO (red)

Source: Puebla region, central valley of Mexico (Mexico City region), and California. Heat: 3

ROCOTILLO

Related to the habanero, Scotch bonnet, and the Jamaican hot. Also known as the *rocoto* and sometimes called a squash pepper because of its resemblance to pattypan squash. Orange-yellow or deep red in its ripe form, rounded in shape with furrows, tapering to a point. Measures about 1 inch long and 1¼ to 1¾ inches in diameter. Thin fleshed, with a mild fruitiness and an intense heat. Very good in ceviches, and pickled (en escabeche). A good addition to salsas.

SANTA FE GRANDE

A type of güero chile. Pale yellow, tapering from broad shoulders, measuring about 2½ inches long and 1¼ to 1½ inches in diameter. Thick fleshed; has a fresh, very light melon flavor and a refined, sharp heat, similar to a high-quality New Mexico green chile. Mainly used in yellow moles, salsas, and pickled (en escabeche).

ROCOTILLO

Source: South America. Heat: 7-8

SANTA FE GRANDE

Source: Northern Mexico and the Southwest. Heat: 6

SCOTCH BONNET

Closely related to the habanero and the Jamaican hot. Pale yellow-green, orange, or red in color, smaller than the habanero though similar in shape, measuring about 1 to 1½ inches long and 1 to 1½ inches in diameter. Very hot; fruity and smoky flavor. The Scotch bonnet is an essential ingredient in the Jamaican specialty called jerk sauce and in Caribbean curries. It is also used as a condiment sauce.

SERRANO

A bright yet dark green to scarlet when ripe. Cylindrical with a tapered, rounded end; measures about 1 to 2 inches long and ½ to ¾ inches in diameter. Thick fleshed; has a clean biting heat and pleasantly high acidity. Literally "highland" or "mountain," the serrano is the hottest chile commonly available in the United States. Excellent in salsas, pickled (en escabeche), or roasted and used in sauces. Green and red serranos can be used interchangeably, although the red will be somewhat sweeter. Red serranos are often used decoratively. Either can substitute for the Thai chile in the ratio of three fresh serranos to one Thai.

SCOTCH BONNET

Source: Jamaica and other Caribbean islands, and coastal Belize. Heat: 9-10

SERRANO

Source: Mexico and the Southwest. Heat: 7

SWEET PURPLE PEPPER

Bright purple. Tapering to a point from broad shoulders, and measuring about 4 to 5 inches long and 2 to 2½ inches in diameter at the shoulders. Thick fleshed; sweet flavor similar to bell peppers. Used in salads.Can be roasted. Like the Dutch red, this chile is being cultivated in Holland as a specialty produce item.

SWEET PURPLE PEPPER
Source: Holland. Heat: 0-1

TABASCO

Bright orange-red, measuring about
1 to 1½ inches long and ¼ to ½
inches in diameter. Thin fleshed; a
sharp, biting heat, with some stemminess and hints of celery and green
onion. Used almost exclusively
in the famous McIlhenny Tabasco®
pepper sauce.

TEPÍN

Ripe form of a wild chile. Also
known as *chiltepín* or *chiltecpín*. Orange
to reddish-brown in its ripe form,
ovoid or spherical in shape, and
measuring about ¼ inch in diameter. Thin fleshed; its fiery heat tends
to dissipate quickly. It resembles the
wild chiles that were discovered by
Columbus. Its name comes from the
Nahuatl word meaning "flea." Good
in salsas, soups, and stews.

THAI

Bright medium green to red when
ripe. Thin, elongated, and pointed;
measures about 1½ inches long and
¼ inch in diameter. Meaty textured
and thin fleshed with copious seeds
and a lingering heat. Primarily used in
Southeast Asian cooking. Red Thais
are sometimes used decoratively in
salads and noodle dishes. Fresh serrano chiles can be substituted in the
ratio of three serranos to one Thai.

TABASCO

Source: Louisiana, and Central and South America. Heat 9

TEPÍN

*Source: South and Central America and the Southwest,
especially the Sonora Desert and surrounding areas. Heat: 8*

THAI

Source: Thailand, Southeast Asia, and California. Heat: 7-8

DRIED
Seco

DRIED CHILES
(*Chiles Secos*)

Ounce for ounce, a dried chile packs a more potent punch than just about anything else in the kitchen larder. The drying process intensifies and magnifies the flavors of the chile and gives it a higher concentration of natural sugars. The result is that the dried chile tends to have a much more distinctive taste than its fresh counterpart, with flavors that are deep and often quite complex. Dried chiles are an indispensable item at Coyote Cafe: we use them in large quantities, mainly in the preparation of sauces.

When buying dried chiles, select those that are uniform in color and that have deep or brilliant color. Make sure they are not faded, dusty, or dirty and that there are no white spots or other markings that indicate improper drying, disease, or over-long storage. Select unbroken chiles, otherwise the essential oils that are contained in the flesh and that give the chiles their unique flavors will have evaporated. Good quality chiles will have a degree of flexibility, indicating freshness (in other words, the chiles are from a recent crop). They should also have a good aroma, like fresh spices. Store dried chiles (and chile powder) in an airtight container in a cool, dry, dark place. Although it is possible to store them for extended periods of time, it is better to use them within six months. If you do keep them longer, check through them occasionally and discard any that have spoiled.

In Mexican and Southwestern cuisines, dried chiles are usually roasted and rehydrated before they are used. Unless your recipe outlines a different procedure, you can follow these general instructions: Stem and seed the chiles, then place them in a skillet, on a comal, or in a 250-degree oven and dry-roast them for three to four minutes. Shake them once or twice and be careful not to scorch them or else they will taste bitter; this in turn will make the sauce taste bitter. The chiles should then be added to water that has been heated to just below the boiling point — if it is boiling, the chiles will lose flavor. Use just enough water to cover the chiles and press them down with a lid. Allow them to sit for 20 minutes or until they are soft. At this point, you should taste the water to see if it is bitter, discarding it if it is. The chiles can then be used as directed in the recipe.

To make sauces with dried chiles, you should roast and rehydrate the chiles as described above, then purée them in a blender (a blender does a better job than a food processor), adding some of the soaking water as needed. Use plain water if the soaking water was too bitter, or you can add a little tomato juice instead. Follow your recipe, using additional water as needed to achieve the desired consistency.

The most interesting sauces made with dried chiles are like musical chords in that they consist of bass, middle range, and high notes. It is advantageous to learn these "notes" and the ways in which they can be combined, although there are no set rules. The bass notes are created by the roasting or smoking process and these are the earthy, woodsy, or smoky tones. The middle notes are mainly fruit flavors, such as dried cherry or plum, particularly present in dried chiles such as the ancho and

▼▼

the *cascabel*. The high notes are derived from the heat, and from the citrus qualities of chiles.

I have found that, as with the fresh chiles, using a combination of dried chiles adds interest and complexity to sauces. Where a sauce recipe calls for a single type of dried chile, try using a blend of two or three different varieties. The proportions can be 80 percent and 20 percent (or 80-10-10, or even 60-20-20), with the dried chile called for in the recipe in largest quantity. Use the sauce recipes in this book as a starting point; once you have mastered them, you can begin to experiment with different flavor combinations.

Learning about and understanding dried chiles is very much like developing an appreciation for fine wines — it is largely a matter of educating the palate so that it becomes sensitive to the range and depth of flavors present. As with wines, it is helpful to establish a tasting vocabulary that will help you conceptualize the flavors. This vocabulary includes the following flavor descriptors: berry, dried cherry and plum, chocolate, citrus, coffee, fruit, liquorice, prune, raisin, spice, tannin, tea, and tobacco; earthiness, smokiness, stemminess, and woodsiness. Mastering this vocabulary will also help you match wines with dishes containing dried chiles. In general you would select a wine that could be described in similar terms as the chile it is to accompany.

If you become as absorbed in the world of dried chiles as I have, here's something you'll enjoy. Gather together a selection of five to ten chiles and invite some friends over for a chile-tasting party!

AJÍ AMARILLO

Orange, wrinkled, tapering to a point, and measuring about 4 inches long and ¾ inch across. Thin fleshed; has a fruity flavor with berry tones. Used in sauces and stews.

AJÍ MIRASOL

Also known as *ají amarillo*, *cusqueño*, or *kellu-uchu*. Usually a deep yellowish red, tapering to a point, and measuring about 3 to 5 inches long and 1 to 1½ inches across. Medium fleshed; has a berrylike fruit flavor. This chile is used to make yellow mole sauces. It is also used in ceviches and salsas, and as a condiment.

AJÍ PANCA

Dark brown, wrinkled, tapering to a point, and measuring about 3 to 5 inches long and 1 to 1½ inches across. Medium fleshed; has a berry flavor with fruit tones. Commonly used in making chile sauces and in fish dishes.

AJÍ AMARILLO
Source: South America, especially Peru. Heat 7-8

AJÍ MIRASOL
Source: South America. Heat: 2.5

AJÍ PANCA
Source: South America, especially Peru. Heat: 1.5

ANCHO

The ancho is a dried poblano chile, and is the most commonly used dried chile in Mexico. Brick red to dark mahogany, with an orange-red cordovan tint when held up to the light. Wrinkled, with broad shoulders (in Spanish, *ancho* means wide), tapering to a round end. Measures 4 to 5 inches long and about 3 inches across at the shoulders. Medium thick fleshed; at its best when very flexible and aromatic. The ancho is the sweetest of the dried chiles. It has a mild fruit flavor with tones of coffee, liquorice, tobacco, dried plum, and raisin, with a little woodsiness. It is frequently mislabeled as a pasilla. The ancho together with the mulato and the true pasilla form the "holy trinity" of chiles used to prepare the traditional mole sauces. The ancho is sold in three grades of quality in Mexico; *primero* is the highest grade and consists of the largest, thickest-fleshed chiles (pictured opposite). *Mediano* is the medium grade, while *ancho* is the basic grade. Indispensable for making sauces and moles. Can be purchased in powdered form.

ANCHO

Source: Puebla region, central valley of Mexico (Mexico City region), and California, Heat: 3-5

CASCABEL

Also known as the *chile bola*. Named for the rattling sound it makes when shaken (in Spanish, *cascabel* means rattle). Dark reddish brown, smooth, and round in shape, measuring about 1½ inches in diameter. Thick fleshed and medium-hot, with a slightly acidic and tannic quality. The rich flavors are a little smoky and woodsy with tobacco and nutty tones, rather like an old red Bordeaux. The tannic heat is noticeable at the back of the throat. Wonderful in salsas, sauces, soups, and stews.

CATARINA

Like the cascabel, the seeds of the *catarina* rattle when shaken. Garnet in color, teardrop or bullet shaped, sometimes tapering to a point, and measuring about 1½ to 2 inches long and ¾ inch across. Thin fleshed; has a mellow rounded heat and a clean crisp flavor with wild berry and tobacco tones. Ideal in spicy salsas, stews, and soups.

CASCABEL

Source: Central Mexico. Heat: 4

CATARINA

*Source: Central and northern Mexico, and southern Texas.
Heat: 5*

CAYENNE

Also known as a Ginnie pepper. Translucent, bright red, tapering to a point, and measuring about 2 to 4 inches long and about ½ inch across. Thin fleshed; very pungent heat, with an acidic, tart flavor and smoky, dusty tones. Both the *chile de árbol* and the *guajillo* are types of cayenne. Dried cayennes can be used in sauces and soups, in bottled sauces, and decoratively. For the most part, though, cayennes are used in powdered form as a seasoning.

CHILHUACLE AMARILLO

Related to the *chilhuacle negro* and *chilhuacle rojo* chiles. Grown only in the south of Mexico. Dark amber to reddish yellow in color, broad shouldered and tapering to a point. Measures about 2 to 3 inches long and 1½ inches across at the shoulders. Medium thick fleshed, with a tart heat. The complex flavor is a little salty and acidic, with bitter orange and sour cherry tones, some melon and seediness, and sweetness in the finish. Mainly used to prepare yellow moles and other sauces.

CAYENNE

Source: Louisiana, Mexico, Asia, and Africa. Heat: 8

CHILHUACLE AMARILLO

Source: Oaxaca and Chiapas. Heat: 4

CHILHUACLE NEGRO

This prized and very expensive chile is grown, like the related *chilhuacle amarillo*, only in southern Mexico. Shiny, dark mahogany in color, and shaped like a miniature bell pepper or almost heart shaped. Measures about 2 to 3 inches long and the same across at the shoulders. One of the most flavorful of all chiles, it has a deep, intense fruit flavor, with tones of dried plum, tobacco, and liquorice, and a subtle, spicy heat. Used to make the black mole sauces that are a specialty of the Oaxaca region.

CHILHUACLE ROJO

Like the *chilhuacle amarillo* and *chilhuacle negro*, this chile is grown exclusively in southern Mexico. Dark red to mahogany in color, and either shaped like a miniature bell pepper or broad shouldered and tapering to a point. Measures about 2 to 3 inches long and 1½ inches across at the shoulders. Richer and deeper flavors than the *chilhuacle amarillo*, with tones of dried figs, liquorice and a hint of wild cherry. Has a medium, sweet heat. It is used in the preparation of certain special mole sauces.

CHILHUACLE NEGRO
Source: Oaxaca and Chiapas. Heat: 4-5

CHILHUACLE ROJO
Source: Oaxaca and Chiapas. Heat: 3

CHILCOSTLE

Bright deep orange-red with a splotchy skin. Elongated and tapered, measuring about 3 to 5 inches long and ½ to ¾ inch across at the shoulders. Thin fleshed, with a dusty, dry medium heat and an orangey sweetness with hints of allspice and fennel. Used in salsas, soups, tamales, and mole sauces.

CHILTEPE

Bright orange-red, thin, usually curved, and tapering to a point. Measures about 2 inches long and ¼ to ⅜ inch across at the shoulders. Thin fleshed; has a dry hay flavor, with nutty and sun-dried tomato tones, and a sharp, searing heat on the tip of the tongue. Primarily used in making sauces and pestos.

CHILCOSTLE
Source: Oaxaca. Heat: 5

CHILTEPE
Source: Oaxaca. Heat: 6

CHIPOTLE

A large, dried, smoked jalapeño;
also known as a *chile ahumado* or a
chile meco. Dull tan to a coffee brown
in color, veined and ridged, measuring about 2 to 4 inches long and
about 1 inch across. Medium thick
fleshed, smoky and sweet in flavor
with tobacco and chocolate tones, a
Brazilnut finish, and a subtle, deep,
rounded heat. As much as one-fifth
of the Mexican jalapeño crop is
processed as *chipotles*. Used mainly in
soups, salsas, and sauces. Chipotles
are widely used in Mexican and
Southwestern cooking. They are
available canned in a red adobo
sauce. The *chipotle grande*, a smoked
dried *huachinango* chile (see Huachi-
nango in the section on fresh chiles),
has similar flavors, but is larger.

COSTEÑO

Related to the *guajillo* chile; also
known as a *chile bandeño*. Orange-red
in color, tapering to a point, and
measuring about 2 to 3 inches long
and ½ to ¾ inch across at the
shoulders. Thin to medium fleshed;
has dusty, green, soapy flavors with
apricot fruit tones and a fiery, intense, lingering heat. Good in salsas,
sauces, and soups.

CHIPOTLE

Source: Veracruz, Oaxaca, Chihuahua, Texas, and southern
New Mexico. Heat: 5-6

COSTEÑO

Source: Guerrero and Oaxaca. Heat: 6-7

COSTEÑO AMARILLO

Shiny, amber in color, tapering to a point, and measuring about 2 to 3 inches long and ¾ to 1 inch across at the shoulders. Wafer-thin flesh; has a light, crisp, lemon-citrus flavor with green tomato and grassy tones, and a subtle heat. Used in the preparation of yellow mole sauces. Also good in soups and stews.

DE ÁRBOL

Literally "treelike," it is a lush plant with thick woody stems. Closely related to the *pico de pajaro* and the cayenne chiles. Bright brick-red, elongated and pointed, measuring about 2 to 3 inches long and ¼ to ⅜ inch across. Thin fleshed; has a tannic, smoky, and grassy flavor, and a searing, acidic heat on the tip of the tongue. Primarily used in powdered form to make sauces. Also used in soups and stews.

COSTEÑO AMARILLO
Source: Guerrero And Oaxaca. Heat: 4

DE ÁRBOL
*Source: Jalisco, Nayarit, and the central valley of Mexico
(Mexico City region).* Heat: 7.5

GUAJILLO

Related to the *pulla*. One of the most
common cultivars grown in Mexico.
Shiny, deep orange-red with brown
tones, elongated, tapering to a point
and sometimes slightly curved.
Measures about 4 to 6 inches long
and 1 to 1½ inches across. Thin
fleshed; has a green tea and stemmy
flavor with berry tones. A little piney
and tannic, with a sweet heat. Commonly used in salsas, chile sauces,
soups, and stews.

GUAJILLO
Source: Mainly northern and central Mexico. Heat: 2-4

HABANERO

Dried form of the fresh habanero. Yellow-orange in color, lantern shaped, measuring about 1½ to 2 inches long and about 1 inch across. Very thin fleshed, with tropical fruit flavors of coconut and papaya, a hint of berry, and an intense, fiery acidic heat. Used mainly in sauces.

HUNGARIAN CHERRY PEPPER

Reddish-mahogany in color and wrinkled. Round, measuring about 1½ to 2 inches in circumference. Thin fleshed with a lot of seeds; light fruity and peppery flavors. Used to flavor stews and to make sauces.

HABANERO

Source: Yucatán and the Caribbean. Heat: 10

HUNGARIAN CHERRY PEPPER

Source: Hungary, Eastern Europe, and California.
Heat: 1-3

MORA

Also known as *mora rojo*. Like the *chipotle* chile, the *mora* is a type of dried, smoked jalapeño. Reddish brown in color, tapered and wrinkled, and measuring about 2 inches long and ½ to ¾ inch wide. Medium fleshed; has a sweet mesquite wood flavor with strong tobacco and plum tones. Has a medium heat that is somewhat lingering. The *mora grande* is a larger version of this chile. It is brownish black in color, measures about 2½ to 3 inches long, and has similar flavor characteristics. Can be used in salsas and sauces.

MORITA

Like the larger *mora*, the *morita* is a type of dried smoked jalapeño. Bright orange-red to red-brown, tapered, and measuring about 1 to 2 inches long and ⅜ inch across. Medium fleshed; has a light, sweet, smoky flavor, with tones of plum, fig, and tea and some tannin. The *morita rayada grande* is a slightly larger version of this chile. It has similar flavor characteristics. Both are used in salsas and sauces.

MORA

Source: Veracruz, Oaxaca, and Chihuahua. Heat: 6

MORITA

Source: Veracruz, Oaxaca, and Chihuahua. Heat: 6.5

MULATO

Like the ancho, the mulato is a type of dried poblano. A deep, dark chocolate brown, but medium-brown when held up to the light. Rounded shoulders, usually tapering to a point, and measuring about 4 to 5 inches long and 2 to 3 inches across. Medium thick fleshed; has a smokier flavor than the ancho, without the depth or lingering taste. While the predominant tone is liquorice, there are hints of dried cherry, tobacco, and horehound. Like the ancho, the mulato is sold in three grades of quality in Mexico; *primero* is the largest and most expensive, *mediano* is the medium grade, and *mulato* refers to the regular, most commonly available form. An essential ingredient in making the classic mole sauce. Can also be used in preparation of soups, stews, and other sauces.

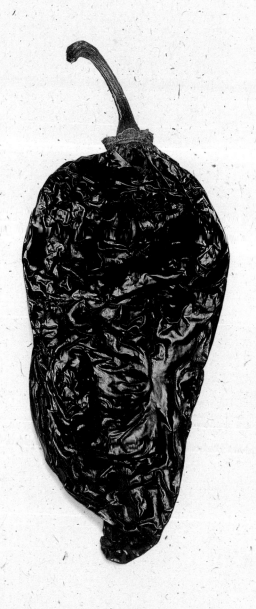

MULATO

Source: Central Mexico. Heat: 2-4

NEW MEXICO
(*green*)

The peeled, dried, roasted form of
the fresh New Mexico green chile,
also referred to as the dried California chile. Medium olive to dark
green in color, flat and tapered,
measuring about 4 to 5 inches long
and 1 inch across. Very thin fleshed;
has a sweet, light, smoky flavor with
hints of citrus and dried apple, and
tones of herbs and celery. It is used
in powdered form to season beef
jerky. Also used in soups and stews.

NEW MEXICO (*green*)
Source: *Rio Grande Valley, New Mexico. Heat: 3-5*

NEW MEXICO
(*red*)

Also known as the *chile colorado* and as the dried California chile. Bright scarlet, elongated, and tapered, measuring about 5 to 7 inches long and 1½ to 2 inches across. Very thin fleshed; has an aroma that is wild and a little sagey. Earthy flavors, with a brickiness, some acidity and weediness, and tones of dried cherry. The heat is crisp and clear. Indispensable in making certain traditional red chile sauces. Also used decoratively in ristras. These chiles are sold in large quantity in the form of crushed flakes and ground chile powders.

NEW MEXICO (*red*)
Source: Rio Grande Valley, New Mexico. Heat: 2-4

NEW MEXICO
(NuMex Eclipse)

A decorative chile, available commercially as NuMex Eclipse. Dark brown in color, elongated, and tapered, measuring about 5 to 7 inches long and 1½ inches across. Similar in flavor to the dried New Mexico red chile. Primarily used as a decorative in ristras.

NEW MEXICO (*NuMex Eclipse*)
Source: Rio Grande Valley, New Mexico. Heat: 2-3

NEW MEXICO
(*NuMex Sunrise*)

A decorative chile, available commercially as NuMex Sunrise. Bright yellow-gold, elongated, and tapered, measuring about 5 to 7 inches long and 1½ inches across. Similar in flavor to the dried New Mexico red chile. Primarily used as a decorative in ristras.

NEW MEXICO (NuMex Sunrise)
Source: Rio Grande Valley, New Mexico. Heat: 2-3

NEW MEXICO
(*NuMex Sunset*)

A decorative chile, available commercially as NuMex Sunset. Bright orange in color, elongated, and tapered, measuring about 5 to 6 inches long and 1 inch across. Similar in flavor to the dried New Mexico red chile. Mainly used as a decorative in ristras.

NEW MEXICO (*NuMex Sunset*)
Source: Rio Grande Valley, New Mexico. Heat: 2-3

NEW MEXICO MINIATURES

In response to a demand for smaller decorative chiles, these special hybrids were developed at New Mexico State University. They are similar in shape and color to the larger decorative New Mexico chiles (see preceding pages), but measure only 2 to 3 inches long and about ½ inches across. Mainly used to make small chile wreaths and ristras.

NEW MEXICO MINIATURES

Source: Southern New Mexico. Heat: 2-3

ONZA

Rare chile. Bright brick-red, tapered, and measuring about 3 inches long and ½ inch across. Thin-fleshed; slightly sweet and also slightly acidic, with flavors of carrot and tomato, and a crisp heat noticeable at the back of the throat. Mainly used in sauces and soups.

PASADO

A New Mexico red or Anaheim red chile that has been roasted, peeled, and dried. Traditionally prepared in this manner by the Pueblo Indians for use during the winter months. A dull, dark orange-red, tapered, and measuring about 4 to 5 inches long and 1 inch across. Thin fleshed; sweeter than the dried New Mexico red; has a dusty, toasty flavor with sweet, ripe apple tones and hints of liquorice and cherry. Leaves a sharp, lingering heat on the front of the tongue. Used to flavor soups, stews, and breads.

ONZA
Source: Oaxaca. Heat: 4-5

PASADO
Source: Rio Grande Valley, New Mexico. Heat: 5

PASILLA

Also known as the *chile negro*. Literally "little raisin," the pasilla is a dried *chilaca* chile. There is some confusion over the name of this chile: in California and northern Mexico, the fresh poblano and its dried forms, the ancho and mulato, are referred to (mistakenly) as pasillas. Dark raisin brown, wrinkled, elongated, and tapering. Measures about 5 to 6 inches long and 1 to 1½ inches across. Thin fleshed; has some berry, grape, and herbaceous tones, and a hint of liquorice. Like the ancho and the mulato, the pasilla is sold in three grades of quality in Mexico: *primero*, *mediano*, and the regular *pasilla*. Together with the ancho and mulato, the pasilla is one of the "holy trinity" of chiles used in the preparation of the traditional mole sauce. It is excellent for making other sauces, especially for seafood. Also used in powdered form.

PASILLA

Source: Guanajuato, Jalisco, and Zacatecas (central
Mexico). Heat: 3-5

PASILLA DE OAXACA

A smoked chile grown only in the Oaxaca region. Shiny red-mahogany in color, very wrinkled, tapered, and measuring about 3 to 4 inches long and 1 to 1½ inches across. Thin fleshed; has an acrid fruit-smoke flavor with strong tobacco tones and a sharp, lingering heat. Mainly used for the rellenos that are a regional specialty.

PASILLA DE OAXACA
Source: Oaxaca. Heat: 6-7

PÁTZCUARO

Related to the pasilla. Deep oxblood red in color, wrinkled, elongated, and tapering to a point. Measures about 4 to 6 inches long and 1 inch across. Thin to medium fleshed; has tea and orange flavors, with a hint of smokiness and green stemminess, and a thin, dry, transient heat. Used in salsas, sauces, and soups.

PEPPERONCINI

Orange-red, wrinkled, tapered, and usually curved. Measures about 2 to 3 inches long and ½ inch across. Thin fleshed with sweet tones. Commonly used as a flavoring for tomato sauces and seafood dishes in southern Europe.

PÁTZCUARO

Source: Pátzcuaro (Michoacán). Heat: 5-6

PEPPERONCINI

Source: Sardinia, Southern Italy, and the southern United
States, especially Louisiana. Heat: 5

PEQUÍN

Also known as *chile pequeño* or *chile piquin* and related to the *tepín*, which is the wild form. Light orange-red, usually oval or shaped like an arrowhead. Measures about ½ to ¾ inch long and ¼ inch across. Thin fleshed; has a light, sweet, smoky flavor with citrus, corn, and nutty tones. Has a deep, fiery, transient heat, slightly more intense than the tepín. Used in making salsas, soups, sauces, and vinegars.

PICO DE PAJARO

Literally "bird's beak," due to the resemblance in shape. Closely related to the *chile de árbol*. Deep orange-red, tapering to a point, and measuring about 1 inch long and ¼ inch across. Thin fleshed, with fruity plum tones. Commonly used in salsas, sauces, marinades, and pickled (en escabeche).

PEQUÍN

Source: South and central America, Mexico, and the Southwest. Heat: 8.5

PICO DE PAJARO

Source: Northern and central Mexico. Heat: 6-7

PULLA

Related to the *guajillo*. Shiny, ox-blood red, curved, elongated, and tapering to a point. Measures about 4 to 5 inches long and ¾ inch across. Thin fleshed; has a light flavor containing sharp fruit and cherry tones with a hint of liquorice. Has a dry, dusty, intense heat. An excellent seasoning for salsas and stews.

SERRANO SECO

A dried serrano chile. Also known as *chile seco*. Orange-red, tapering to a point, and measuring about 1½ to 2 inches long and ½ inch across. Thin fleshed; has fruit and citrus flavors, and an intense heat. Primarily used in sauces. Also used in powdered form.

PULLA

Source: Central valley of Mexico (Mexico City region).
Heat: 6

SERRANO SECO

Source: Veracruz and central valley of Mexico (Mexico City
region). Heat: 7.5

SERRANO SECO DE YUCATÁN

A regional variation of the *serrano seco* or *chile seco*. Faded yellowish orange, tapering to a point, measuring about 1½ to 2 inches long and ½ to ¾ inch across. Very thin fleshed; has a tart, bitter, and rather tannic flavor with grassy tones. Leaves a strong, lingering heat on the front of the tongue. Used in powdered form as a seasoning. Also used in salsas.

TEPÍN

Also known as *chiltepín* or *chiltecpín*. A wild form of the *pequín*. (See also *Tepín* in the section on fresh chiles.) Medium red, ovoid or spherical in shape, and measuring about ½ inch across. Thin fleshed; has a dry and dusty flavor and a searing, transient heat. Very good in salsas, soups, stews, and flavored vinegars.

TUXTLA

A type of *pequín* chile. Orange-amber, shaped like a small arrowhead or an elongated heart, and measuring about ¾ inch long and ¼ to ½ inch across. Very thin fleshed; has a dusty, dry, straw flavor and a sharp, dry, lingering heat. Mainly used in salsas.

SERRANO SECO DE YUCATÁN

Source: Yucatán and Veracruz. Heat: 7.5

TEPÍN

*Source: South and Central America, and the Southwest
(especially the Sonora Desert and surrounding area). Heat: 8*

TUXTLA

Source: Southern Mexico. Heat: 7

RECIPES

A RISTRA OF
CHILE RECIPES

I chose the recipes in this section to give you, the reader, the broadest possible introduction to my good friend, the chile. So in this small collection of recipes, you will find some basic sauces and salsas that are relatively easy to prepare, together with some dishes that are fairly complicated. In all, they demonstrate how to use many different chiles, both fresh and dried, in many different applications, with a variety of foods — and all with wonderfully flavorful and exciting results.

We use all these recipes at Coyote Cafe. The versions presented here have been scaled down and adapted to home cooking. Some of the recipes have existed in similar form for thousands of years in Mexico or the Southwest, while others are more modern or have come from other regions. These recipes generally call for the most commonly available types of chiles, and include some alternative suggestions in those cases where the chiles are less easy to obtain.

If you are unfamiliar with chiles, use these recipes to start you on your journey down the road to adventure. You may need a little daring to begin with, but you'll find it was well worth it because a knowledge of chiles is a culinary tool that will make your cooking come alive. You'll find that a judicious use of chiles will make a world of difference in the foods you prepare.

I recommend learning to use chiles first for flavor, and then for heat. As you become acquainted with the many uses of chiles and their different personalities, you will become comfortable working with them. You may even want to start growing your own chiles, or researching the various sources of chiles (page 155), or hunting for more chile recipes to extend your repertoire. When you reach that point, you will then have officially joined me as a true chile aficionado.

CHIPOTLES IN ADOBO SAUCE

Chipotles in adobo are chipotles that have been stewed in a lightly seasoned liquid. They have become very popular in Southwestern cooking because they provide a distinctive warm heat and delicious smoky flavor. They can be added to almost anything, including breads, sauces, salad dressings, and pastas. I use them in many of my own creations, as you will note even in the small collection of recipes included in this book. Although you can buy canned chipotles in adobo (you can find them in markets that specialize in Latin-American foods), this homemade alternative is far superior and is very easy to prepare. It can also be made with other smoked, dried chiles such as pasillas de Oaxaca, mora grandes, or moritas.

Yield: 1 cup

7 to 10 medium-sized dried chipotle chiles, stemmed and slit lengthwise
⅓ cup onion, cut into ½-inch slices
5 tablespoons cider vinegar
2 cloves garlic, sliced
4 tablespoons ketchup
¼ teaspoon salt
3 cups water

Combine all ingredients in a pan, cover, and cook over very low heat for 1 to 1½ hours, until the chiles are very soft and the liquid has reduced down to 1 cup. This recipe will keep for several weeks in the refrigerator in an airtight container. For chipotle purée, place cooked chipotles and sauce in a blender, and purée. Put through a fine sieve to remove seeds.

CARIBE SALSA

This salsa contains tropical fruity tones that are perfectly complemented by the habanero or Scotch bonnet chile. You can use mangoes, papayas, or other tropical fruit instead of (or as well as) the pineapple, and mint instead of basil, if you prefer. Habaneros are available in specialty produce stores (or see the list of sources in the back of the book). This salsa goes best with grilled fish, seafood (especially lobster), or grilled chicken.

Yield: About 2 cups

2 tablespoons diced onion
2 cups tomatoes cut into ¼-inch dice
1 fresh habanero or Scotch bonnet chile, seeded and finely minced
4 tablespoons basil, julienned
1 small red bell pepper, cut into ¼-inch dice
juice of 2 limes or 1 bitter orange
½ cup diced fresh ripe pineapple
½ teaspoon salt

Put onion in a strainer, rinse with hot water, and drain. Combine all ingredients and mix well. Let sit in the refrigerator for at least 30 minutes before serving. Serve cool.

ROASTED CORN SALSA

In this unusual salsa, the woodsy flavors of wild mushrooms complement the taste of roasted corn, while the poblanos contribute the fire. This is one of Coyote Cafe's most versatile recipes, as it goes well with just about everything. We serve it with grilled chicken, venison sausage, chiles rellenos, cheese enchiladas, and corn crêpes with goat cheese. It can also be used as a vegetable dish. If fresh wild mushrooms are not available use a combination of dried wild and fresh domestic mushrooms.

Yield: About 3 cups

5 ears fresh corn

3/8 cup fresh morels or other wild mushrooms, cleaned and diced

4 teaspoons extra virgin olive oil

1/4 cup sun-dried tomatoes, finely diced, with 1 teaspoons of their oil

2 large poblano chiles, roasted, peeled, seeded, and diced

2 teaspoons minced marjoram

1 clove garlic, roasted, peeled, and chopped

1 teaspoon adobo sauce from chipotle chiles in adobo sauce

1/2 teaspoon sherry vinegar

1 teaspoon fresh Mexican lime juice

1/2 teaspoon kosher salt

With a sharp knife cut corn kernels from the cobs. Heat a heavy-bottomed sauté pan over high heat until almost smoking. Place no more than two layers of kernels in the pan at a time, and dry-roast for about 5 minutes until smoky and dark, tossing continuously.

Sauté mushrooms in 1/2 teaspoon of the oil until well cooked, about 10 minutes. Mix corn, mushrooms, remaining oil, and the rest of the ingredients together. Serve salsa at room temperature or warm.

GREEN CHILE CHUTNEY

This is very easy to make, and it goes particularly well with crab cakes (we always seem to run out of both when we serve them at Coyote Cafe!). It also goes well with eggs, pork, chicken, and sautéed trout or salmon. It can be served warm or cold. In short, it makes sense to have this chutney around, just in case! (Store it in the refrigerator—it keeps very well.)

Yield: 4 cups

2 pounds fresh New Mexico green chiles, roasted, peeled, and diced (or roasted Anaheim chiles, with 2 or 3 roasted jalapeños)
2 cups sugar
1 tablespoon roasted ground Mexican oregano
⅔ cup cider vinegar
1 teaspoon salt

Mix the ingredients together and cook for 10 to 15 minutes over medium heat in an enamel or stainless steel pan. Allow to cool, and serve cold. For a hotter chutney, add 6 diced roasted jalapeños (or increase the number accordingly if using Anaheims and jalapeños).

GUAJILLO SALSA

Guajillos are one of the most popular dried chiles in Mexico for making salsas. Its distinctive fruit and citrus qualities and medium heat make it a great accompaniment for all seafood, especially shrimps and scallops. This recipe can be served cold as a salsa or hot as a sauce; either way, be prepared for the compliments to fly!

Yield: 3 cups

½ pound dried guajillo chiles
3 cups water
5 large cloves roasted garlic
1 teaspoon ground cumin
1 teaspoon salt
½ pound Roma tomatoes
2 teaspoons toasted pumpkin seeds
⅓ cup cider vinegar
1 teaspoon roasted ground Mexican oregano

Remove stems from the guajillos. Roast and rehydrate the chiles as described in the introduction to the section on dried chiles. Purée with the remaining ingredients. To use as a sauce, heat 2 tablespoons peanut oil or lard in a high-sided pan and refry sauce at a sizzle for 3 to 5 minutes, stirring continuously. Add a little water if necessary.

MARK'S RED CHILE SAUCE

This is my own version of New Mexico's most famous sauce. It has no rough edges, as so many sauces do. Instead, it is a round, smooth, deep sauce given extra dimensions by the combination of different types of red chiles it contains. Serve it with complex, hearty dishes, such as venison, red meats, grilled food, and enchiladas. For good results, it is important that you use chiles of high quality.

Yield: 4 cups

4 ounces whole dried New Mexico red chiles
2 ounces whole dried ancho chiles
2 ounces whole dried cascabel chiles
2 whole dried chipotle chiles or chipotles in adobo sauce
1 teaspoon adobo sauce
2 quarts water
1 pound Roma tomatoes
1/2 cup chopped white onion
1 tablespoon olive oil
5 large cloves garlic, roasted, peeled, and finely chopped
1 teaspoon roasted ground cumin
1 1/2 teaspoons roasted ground Mexican oregano
1 teaspoon salt
2 tablespoons peanut oil or lard

Remove stems and seeds from chiles. Roast and rehydrate the chiles as described in the introduction to the section on dried chiles.

Blacken the tomatoes in a skillet or under a broiler (about 5 minutes). Sauté onion in the oil over low heat until browned. Put chiles in a blender and add blackened tomatoes, onion, garlic, cumin, oregano, and salt. Add 1 cup of the reserved liquid. (Taste the chile water first; if it is not bitter, use it. Otherwise, add plain water or chicken stock.) Purée to a fine smooth paste, adding more chile water, water, or chicken stock if necessary.

Add oil or lard to a high-sided pan, and heat until almost smoking. Refry sauce at a sizzle for 3 to 5 minutes, stirring continuously. Do not allow sauce to get too thick; add water if necessary. Sauce can be kept for up to 1 week in the refrigerator.

JALAPEÑO KETCHUP

This is an old Southwestern favorite that gives extra zing to homemade French fries, burgers, and eggs — or whatever else you put ketchup on! Most regular ketchups are too sweet and too mild. I like this version, which has been perfected by Mark Kiffin, the head chef at Coyote Cafe. It exemplifies my belief that chiles make everything better.

Yield: 3 to 4 cups

1 medium onion
1 tablespoon olive oil
½ cup sugar
2 teaspoons cumin seed, toasted and ground
1 tablespoon toasted oregano
1 cup rice vinegar
2 roasted jalapeño chiles, minced
1 cup Mark's Red Chile Sauce
2 cups roasted Roma tomatoes, pureed
½ large bunch cilantro, chopped
salt to taste

In a large saucepan, sauté onion lightly in olive oil until soft. Add the sugar and cook to a glaze, about 5 minutes. Add the cumin and oregano, deglaze with the vinegar, and reduce slightly. Add the jalapeños, Red Chile Sauce, tomatoes, and cilantro. Simmer over low heat for about 1 hour. Allow to cool, and then purée. Season with salt to taste. Add water if ketchup becomes too thick or tastes too hot.

GREEN CHILE SAUCE

This sauce can vary from mild to scorching, depending on the strength of the chiles used. For the best results, make the sauce with fresh roasted New Mexico green chiles. In my opinion, the best green chiles in the world come from New Mexico, due to its unique altitude and climate. The roasting process provides one of the great fall aromas in Santa Fe. Huge burlap sacks of New Mexico chiles are emptied into large butane-fired drums, and the drums are turned by hand so that the torches flame and char the skins; the air becomes thick with fiery oils. If fresh or frozen New Mexico green chiles are unavailable, use a combination of fresh Anaheim and jalapeño or serrano chiles. This sauce goes well with the simple flavors of eggs, potatoes, or chicken, and makes a great base for Green Chile Stew.

Yield: 4 cups

4 pounds fresh New Mexico green chiles (or Anaheim chiles with 3 or 4 jalapeños or serranos)

8 cloves garlic, roasted, peeled, and finely chopped

4 cups water

4 teaspoons roasted Mexican oregano (rubbed between the fingers, but not too fine)

1 teaspoon roasted ground cumin

2 teaspoons salt

Roast the chiles under the broiler for about 5 minutes, until lightly blackened. Place in a plastic bag or closed container and allow to "sweat" and cool. Remove the blackened parts without washing (to preserve the oils). Place the chile and the rest of the ingredients in a food processor and chop at a medium setting (do not purée). Warm before serving.

MANGO-HABANERO SAUCE

Mark Kiffin, the head chef at Coyote Cafe, developed this recipe after we had tried a similar sauce made by Robbin Haas at the Veranda at Turnberry Isle in North Miami. It proves the point that a barbecue sauce does not have to be heavy and tomatoey; this one is quite refined, though very spicy. The tropical tones of the mangoes combined with the habanero chiles perfectly offset delicate, rich seafood such as lobster or scallops. It can also be used as a barbecue sauce, and proves its versatility at Coyote Cafe where we also serve it with Crab Rellenos as well as with grilled pork.

Yield: About 3 cups

2 tablespoons peanut oil
3 ripe mangoes, peeled and cut into large dice
½ cup diced white onion
½ cup diced carrot
2 fresh orange habanero chiles
½ cup champagne vinegar
½ cup ketchup
¼ cup sugar
salt to taste

Heat the oil in a saucepan and add mangoes, onion, carrot, and habanero chiles. Cook for about 10 minutes over medium heat, until onions are soft and translucent. Deglaze with vinegar, and add ketchup and sugar. Bring to a slow boil, reduce heat, and simmer for 35 to 45 minutes. Remove from heat and season with salt to taste. Transfer to a blender, pulse sauce, and strain through a medium strainer. If the sauce is too thick, add a little water to thin.

SMOKED CHILE BARBECUE SAUCE

Most spicy barbecue sauces are made with cayenne or other hot chiles, which provide heat but neither roundness nor an interesting complexity. This recipe contains a wonderfully satisfying combination of flavors, highlighted by the chipotle chiles which lend an essential smoky quality to the sauce. This is a good all-round, all-purpose barbecue sauce that is hot, deep, spicy, and a little sweet. When you use this sauce do not cook over a high fire, as the sauce will caramelize and brown. Instead, marinate the food in the sauce first, then grill it slowly, finishing it over a higher heat. Brush on more sauce to serve.

Yield: 3 to 4 cups

1 cup rice vinegar
1 cup cider vinegar
2 teaspoons ground cloves
1 teaspoon ground allspice
2 tablespoons ground coriander
1 medium onion, diced
1 head roasted garlic, peeled and chopped
¼ cup olive oil
1 cup brown sugar
¼ cup molasses
1 cup chipotle chiles in adobo sauce, puréed
1½ bottles tomato ketchup
1 tablespoon Worcestershire sauce
salt to taste

Mix together the vinegars and spices in a saucepan, and over medium heat reduce by half. In a large pan, sauté onion and garlic lightly in the olive oil until soft. Add the brown sugar and stir in the molasses. Reduce slightly, and then add the vinegar mixture, chipotles, ketchup, and Worcestershire sauce. Cook slowly over low heat for about 1 hour. Season with salt to taste. Strain through a medium sieve, pressing out the juices of the onion and garlic.

TAMARIND CHIPOTLE SAUCE

I created this sauce one evening while cooking ribs over an outdoor barbecue. It is definitely not a traditional sauce, but I really like the smoky hotness of the chipotle chiles combined with the sourness of tamarind. You can buy blocks of tamarind paste from Southeast Asian grocery stores: processing tamarind in this form is much less time consuming than using fresh tamarind pods. This sauce goes very well with any pork dish, especially barbecued pork, or with seafood such as shrimp and soft-shelled crab, especially when combined with a little mint. It can also be used as an interesting variation on Chinese plum sauce.

Yield: 3 cups

a 14-ounce block of tamarind paste
2 cups water
½ cup dark brown sugar
2 cloves garlic, roasted and peeled
2 chipotle chiles in adobo sauce
juice of 1 lime

Add the tamarind paste to the water and heat gently, stirring until smooth. Place in a blender and purée together with the sugar, garlic, chipotles, and adobo sauce. Then add the lime juice and blend in. Serve slightly warmed.

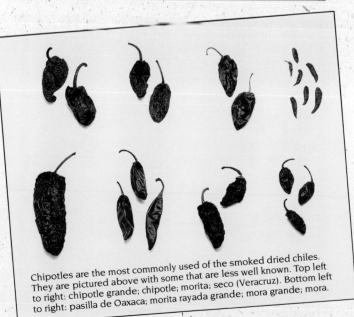

Chipotles are the most commonly used of the smoked dried chiles. They are pictured above with some that are less well known. Top left to right: chipotle grande; chipotle; morita; seco (Veracruz). Bottom left to right: pasilla de Oaxaca; morita rayada grande; mora grande; mora.

PIPIÁN ROJO

Pipiáns are pesto-like sauces made with chiles, ground seeds, and nuts. They date back to pre-Columbian times, as they were known to have been served at court feasts of the Aztec ruler Montezuma. Pipiáns can be served with appetizers, or used as a sandwich spread, in stuffings, or as a sauce or garnish for grilled meats. This red pipián gets its color from the dried ancho and guajillo chiles, and also from the tomatoes.

Yield: 5 cups

2 ounces whole dried ancho chiles
2 ounces whole dried guajillo chiles
1 quart water
¾ pound Roma tomatoes
½ cup finely chopped white onion
2 tablespoons olive oil
4 ounces green unroasted pumpkin seeds (about
    1 heaping cup)
6 cloves garlic, roasted and peeled
2 chipotle chiles in adobo sauce
1 teaspoon adobo sauce
½ cup dry-roasted peanuts
½ teaspoon ground allspice
2 teaspoons canela (or 1 teaspoon cinnamon)
pinch ground cloves
1 teaspoon sugar
1½ teaspoons salt
1 teaspoon duck fat (or peanut oil)

Remove stems and seeds from ancho and guajillo chiles. Roast and rehydrate the chiles as described in the introduction to the section on dried chiles.

Blacken tomatoes in a skillet or under a broiler (about 5 minutes). Sauté onion in the oil over low heat until slightly browned. Dry-roast pumpkin seeds in a sauté pan for about 5 minutes until they have finished popping. Place in a blender and purée together with tomatoes to form a paste. Add the chiles, about ½ cup of chile water if it is not bitter (otherwise use plain water), onion, garlic, chipotles, adobo sauce, peanuts, spices, sugar, and salt, and purée further.

Add duck fat or oil to a high-sided pan, and heat until almost smoking. Refry sauce at a sizzle for 3 to 5 minutes, stirring continuously. Serve at room temperature.

PIPIÁN VERDE

This green pipián sauce contains a base of fresh greens, fresh herbs, and poblano chiles. In Mexico, Pipián Verde is made with the yerba santa leaf, which has a strong sassafras-like flavor, similar to root beer. This recipe uses anise seed instead. This sauce is traditionally served with roast duck or duck enchiladas, but it also goes very well with pork or scallops or it can be tossed with pasta. It can be served together with Pipián Rojo to create an attractive combination of flavors and colors.

Yield: 4 cups

- 4 ounces green unroasted pumpkin seeds (about 1 heaping cup)
- ½ cup finely chopped white onion
- 2 tablespoons peanut oil
- 1 cup rich chicken stock
- 3 green poblano chiles, roasted, peeled, seeded, and chopped
- 1½ cups cilantro
- 2 cloves garlic, roasted and peeled
- 8 large leaves romaine lettuce, chopped (no stems)
- 1 bunch watercress
- 1 bunch radish tops
- 1½ teaspoons roasted anise seed (or 4 large *yerba santa* leaves, chopped very finely)
- 1 teaspoon salt
- 1 teaspoon sugar
- 1 tablespoon duck fat (or peanut oil)

Dry-roast pumpkin seeds in a sauté pan for about 5 minutes until they have finished popping. Set aside a few seeds for garnish. Sauté onion in the oil over low heat until slightly browned. Process the pumpkin seeds, stock, and poblano chiles in a blender to form a paste. Add ½ cup cilantro and the remaining ingredients, except for the duck fat or oil, and purée.

Add duck fat to a high-sided pan, and heat until almost smoking. Refry sauce at a sizzle for 3 to 4 minutes, stirring continuously; do not overcook or the sauce will lose its greenness. Return to blender, add the remaining cup of cilantro, and purée together. Garnish with the reserved pumpkin seeds. Serve at room temperature. The sauce can be gently warmed, if desired, but be careful not to bring it to a boil or it will its color.

MOLE ROJO

The region of central Mexico that includes Puebla and Oaxaca is known as the Land of Seven Moles: this classic red mole is one of them. Most people in the United States associate moles with a chocolatey sauce, but if there is chocolate in a mole sauce (some moles contain no chocolate at all), it will only be one of many ingredients. The word *mole*, in fact, is a Nahuatl word meaning "mixture." The chocolate used in this recipe balances the sharp acidic flavors of the tomatoes and tomatillos, and the dry fruit ingredients enhance the plum or prune flavors of the ancho and mulato chiles. Mole Rojo is traditionally served with fowl — turkey in particular.

Yield: 5 cups

- 6 whole dried pasilla chiles
- 10 whole dried ancho chiles
- 8 whole dried mulato chiles
- 2 quarts water
- 4 tomatillos
- 5 Roma tomatoes
- ½ cup raisins (or dried plums or dried cherries)
- ⅓ cup sesame seeds
- ½ cup whole almonds, unskinned
- 1 tablespoon peanut oil
- 2 corn tortillas, dried in the oven and chopped
- 6 cloves garlic, roasted and peeled
- 2 cups brown duck stock or chicken stock
- 4 teaspoons canela (or 2 teaspoons cinnamon)
- ⅛ teaspoon ground cloves
- ½ teaspoon ground black pepper
- ½ teaspoon ground allspice
- 1 teaspoon salt
- 3 ounces Mexican Ibarra chocolate
- 2 ounces unsweetened chocolate
- 3 tablespoons duck fat (or peanut oil)

Remove stems and seeds from chiles. Roast and rehydrate the chiles as described in the introduction to the section on dried chiles.

Husk the tomatillos and wash them under hot water. Blacken the tomatillos and tomatoes in a skillet or under a broiler (about 5 minutes). Soak the raisins in warm water until soft (about 20 minutes); discard the water. Dry-roast sesame seeds in a sauté pan for about 5 minutes until they have finished popping; do not allow seeds to burn. Sauté the almonds in the oil over low to medium heat until browned. Purée the tomatillos, tomatoes, sesame seeds, almonds, and tortillas in a blender to form a paste. Add the chiles, raisins, garlic, stock, spices, and salt, and purée together. Melt the chocolate and blend into the mixture.

Add the duck fat to a high-sided pan, and heat until almost smoking. Refry sauce over medium heat for 5 to 15 minutes, stirring constantly. Add more stock if necessary — do not allow to get too thick. Strain the sauce through a sieve, and serve warm, not hot.

The "holy trinity" of chiles used to prepare traditional mole sauces. Left to right: ancho, mulato, pasilla.

MOLE AMARILLO

Moles come in a variety of colors, including red, brown, black, and green. This yellow mole is a specialty of Oaxaca. Its light, spicy flavors with fruit and citrus tones go very well with seafood and chicken, and it is easy to make. Cooking moles in a clay pot will give the sauce a smoother taste; putting them through a strainer gives them a finer texture and helps weave the flavors more closely together.

Yield: About 2 cups

1 large yellow onion
1 tablespoon butter
15 güero chiles, cut in half and seeded
3 yellow bell peppers, roasted and peeled
8 fresh green tomatillos
3 cloves roasted garlic
½ teaspoon cinnamon
½ teaspoon ground allspice
1 teaspoon sugar
pinch nutmeg
salt to taste
2 tablespoons duck fat (or peanut oil)

In a large, thick-bottomed pan, sauté the onions in the butter until soft and sweet but not caramelized. Add the güero chiles and yellow bell peppers, and cook over low heat until soft (about 30 minutes). Husk the tomatillos and wash them under very hot water, or blanch them in boiling water for 15 seconds. Chop the tomatillos and place in a blender together with the onions, chiles, bell peppers, and the remaining ingredients, except for the duck fat or oil. Purée, adding a little water if necessary.

Add duck fat or oil to a high-sided pan, and heat until almost smoking. Refry sauce at a sizzle for 5 to 7 minutes, stirring continuously and allowing the flavors to marry. Adjust seasoning.

TARASCAN BEAN SOUP

This soup's hearty nature is appropriate, given the legendary fierceness of the Taras-can Indians of Michoacán, with whom the dish originated. The Tarascan civilization of the 14th and 15th centuries was one of the few that was never conquered by the Aztecs, and was one of the last in Mexico to fall to the Spanish conquistadores. This version is one of the most popular soups we have ever served at Coyote Cafe.

Yield: 4 servings

½ pound dried red kidney beans (1¼ cups)
2 sprigs epazote, finely chopped (optional)
1 teaspoon salt
2 teaspoons toasted dried oregano
½ large white onion, sliced
1 tablespoon olive oil
1 pound Roma tomatoes
2 cloves roasted garlic
2 tablespoons puréed chipotle in adobo
2 pasilla de Oaxaca chiles (or anchos or mula-tos), stemmed
½ cup peanut oil
8 ounces Monterey jack cheese, cut into 4 slices

Place the beans in a saucepan with the epa-zote, salt, and oregano, and enough water to cover the beans. Cover pan, and bring to a boil. Reduce to a simmer, and cook for about 1½ hours until beans are soft. Stir occasionally, and add more water as necessary.

Preheat oven to 350 degrees. Sauté the onions briefly in olive oil. Cut the tomatoes in half and remove seeds. Place tomatoes on a baking sheet and roast at 350 degrees for 45 minutes. Transfer tomatoes to a blender, add the cooked beans, garlic, onions, chipotle purée, and blend. Add a little water if it seems too thick. Put purée through a medium- to fine-meshed sieve or pass through a food mill, removing seeds and skins.

Heat soup over low heat in a saucepan. Meanwhile, lightly fry the chiles in the peanut oil for a few seconds, just until softened, and then cut into strips. Add slices of cheese and chile strips to the soup and season with salt to taste. When cheese has melted, ladle soup into heated bowls.

SPICY GRILLED SHRIMP AND MELON SALAD

This is one of my favorite brunch dishes. It combines the searing heat of shrimp marinated with chiles de árbol and the refreshing taste of ripe melons. Mint provides the perfect accent in this dish as it combines well with the fruit flavors and contrasts with the heat of the chiles. The secret to making this salad is to cool the grilled shrimp in their shells at room temperature rather than refrigerating them, which can toughen and dry them out, and to peel them at the last minute. Feel free to use any combination of melons: only the watermelon is a must!

Yield: 4 to 6 servings

- 15 dried chiles de árbol (or cayenne chiles)
- 1½ cups olive oil
- 1 teaspoon salt
- 2 cloves garlic, sliced
- 1 bunch cilantro, chopped
- juice of 1 lime
- 30 to 35 medium shrimp, unpeeled and heads removed
- 4 cups watermelon, cantaloupe, and honeydew, cut into ½-inch dice
- 3 tablespoons sugar
- ½ cup finely chopped mint leaves
- juice of 1 lime
- 1 tablespoon rice wine vinegar
- 3 cups romaine, central rib removed, cut into wide strips

Grind the chiles in a spice mill to form a powder (about 2 tablespoons). In a bowl, mix chile powder with oil, salt, garlic, cilantro, and lime juice. Add shrimp and marinate for 2 to 3 hours at room temperature, or overnight in a refrigerator. Combine melons, sugar, mint, lime juice, and vinegar, and refrigerate for at least 30 minutes.

Prepare a hot grill. Remove shrimp from marinade and reserve marinade. Grill shrimp for about 3 minutes, and set aside to cool. Toss the romaine with 4 tablespoons of the reserved marinade, and form a bed of greens on each plate. Drain the melons slightly. Peel the shrimp, toss lightly in some of the reserved marinade. Place melons and shrimp on romaine.

SHRIMP RELLENOS

Relleno is a Spanish word meaning "stuffed"; chiles rellenos are chiles that have been stuffed. Usually, they are filled with cheese, but they can also be stuffed with meat or, as in this recipe, with seafood. This interesting variation on a traditional recipe can be used as an appetizer or as a main dish. Serve Shrimp Rellenos with your favorite salsa or with a fresh tomato and basil sauce.

Yield: 4 servings

2 quarts corn oil
4 fresh New Mexico green chiles
¾ pound fresh shrimp, in the shell
2 ounces Fontina cheese, grated
4 ounces Monterey jack cheese, grated
1 red bell pepper, roasted, peeled, and diced
½ cup fresh corn kernels
3 tablespoons diced white onion
2 tablespoons chopped fresh marjoram
2 tablespoons chopped cilantro
4 eggs, whisked
1 cup medium-grain blue cornmeal

Heat corn oil in a deep-fryer to 375 degrees. Deep-fry chiles for about 3 minutes, or until skin blisters. Place in a stainless steel bowl, cover with plastic wrap, and sweat for 20 minutes. Reserve oil and keep warm.

Grill or dry-roast the shrimp. (To dry-roast, cook briefly on a comal or in a heavy-bottomed skillet without any liquid or fat.) Peel shrimp and chop into large pieces. Combine in a large bowl with the cheeses, bell pepper, corn, onion, and herbs, and mix well. Divide mixture into 4 portions. Gently peel chiles, cut a lengthwise slit in each, and carefully remove seeds. Stuff with shrimp mixture and roll gently between the fingers to close the opening.

Reheat oil to 375 degrees. Dip the chiles in the whisked egg and then roll in the cornmeal. Deep-fry until exterior is dark blue, about 4 to 5 minutes.

For a lighter version, you can make the rellenos without frying them. Just heat the stuffed chiles in a 400-degree oven for about 20 minutes, taking care not to overcook the shrimp.

PORK LOIN
with Cascabel and Grapefruit Sauce

This dish originated in Veracruz on the Mexican Caribbean coast. At first sight this recipe may appear to yield simple flavors, but the cooked citrus juice and allspice create a quite complex taste. Cascabel chiles, literally "little rattles," are round and red, and have a pleasing warmth rather than a fiery heat, thus making excellent sauces.

Yield: 4 servings

- **24 dried cascabel chiles**
- **3 cups water**
- **6 cloves garlic**
- **4 cups fresh grapefruit juice**
- **1 cup fresh orange juice**
- **3 teaspoons allspice**
- **1 teaspoon salt**
- **4 double pork loin chops**
- **4 tablespoons olive oil**

Remove stems and seeds from chiles. With a comal or black iron skillet, or in an oven at 250 degrees, dry roast chiles for 3 to 4 minutes. Shake once or twice and do not allow to blacken. Add to the water in a covered pan and simmer very low for 20 minutes to rehydrate. Allow to cool. Taste the chile water, and if not bitter, add about ½ cup and the chiles to a blender (use plain water if bitter). Purée together with the garlic and strain. Add the fruit juices, allspice, and salt and mix together. Place pork in marinade and refrigerate overnight.

Remove pork and bring to room temperature, and reserve the marinade. In a skillet over high heat, bring olive oil to almost smoking, and reduce heat to medium. Sear pork in olive oil until browned, about 1 to 2 minutes per side. Pour off excess fat and set aside.

Preheat oven to 450 degrees. In an ovenproof pan over medium heat, reduce reserved marinade by one-half. Then add meat and roast in oven for 40 minutes, or until internal temperature reaches 140 degrees. Add a little water to pan if it gets too dry. Serve meat with sauce from pan, and black beans and fried sweet potato chips, if desired.

SOURCES

FRESH AND DRIED CHILES

Coyote Cafe General Store
132 West Water Street, Santa Fe, NM 87501
(505) 982-2454

Josie's,
1130 Agua Fria, Santa Fe, NM 87501
(505) 983-6520

Casados Farms
P.O. Box 1269, San Juan Pueblo, NM 87566
(505) 507-7499

Bueno Foods
2001 Fourth Street, S.W., Albuquerque, NM 87102
(505) 243-2722

Mercado Latino
245 Baldwin Park Blvd., City of Industry, TX 41746
(800) 432-7266

Mi Rancho
464 Seventh Street, Oakland, CA 94607
(510) 451-2393

Casa Lucas Market
2934 24th Street, San Francisco, CA 94110
(415) 826-4334

La Palma
2884 24th Street, San Francisco, CA 94110
(415) 647-1500

Midwest Imports
1121 South Clinton, Chicago, IL 60607
(312) 939-8400

Dean & Deluca
560 Broadway, New York, NY 10012,
(212) 431-1691

The Cool Chile Co.
Dodie Miller Unit 7
34 Bassett Road, London W10 6JL, UK
(081) 968-8898

SEEDS

Plants of the Southwest
Agua Fria, Rte. 6 Box 11A, Santa Fe, NM 87501
(505) 471-2212

Lockhart Seeds Inc.
P.O. Box 1361, Stockton, CA 95201
(209) 466-4401

Exotica Seed Co.
P.O. Box 160, Vista, CA 92083
(619) 724-9093

The Pepper Gal
P.O. Box 12534, Lake Park, FL 33403

W. Atlee Burpee
300 Park Avenue, Warminster, PA 18974
(215) 674-4900

Harris Seeds
P. O. Box 22960, Rochester, NY 14692
(716) 442-0410

Johnny's Selected Seeds
1 Foss Hill Road, Albion, ME 04910
(207) 437-9294

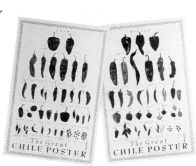